INFORMATION FOR SALE: HOW TO START AND OPERATE YOUR OWN DATA RESEARCH SERVICE

John H. Everett
and
Elizabeth Powell Crowe

TAB BOOKS Inc.

Blue Ridge Summit, PA

FIRST EDITION
FIRST PRINTING

Copyright © 1988 by John H. Everett and Elizabeth Powell Crowe
Printed in the United States of America

Library of Congress Cataloging in Publication Data

Everett, John H.
Information for sale : how to start and operate your own data
research service / by John H. Everett and Elizabeth Powell Crowe.
    p.   cm.
Includes index.
ISBN 0-8306-9357-2 (pbk.)
1. Information services industry—Management. 2. New business
enterprises—Management. 3. Small business—Management. I. Crowe,
Elizabeth Powell. II. Title.
HD9999.I492E86 1988   88-12319
025.1—dc19   CIP

TAB BOOKS Inc. offers software for
sale. For information and a catalog,
please contact TAB Software Department,
Blue Ridge Summit, PA 17294-0850.

TAB books are available at special discounts for bulk purchases for sales
promotions, fund raisers, or premiums. For details, contact: Special Sales Manager, TAB BOOKS Inc., Blue Ridge Summit, PA 17294-0850. 1-800-233-1128
(in Pennsylvania and Alaska call 717-794-2191).

Questions regarding the content of this book
should be addressed to:

Reader Inquiry Branch
TAB BOOKS Inc.
Blue Ridge Summit, PA 17294-0214

Trademarks
and Service Marks

Contents

Foreword

Information brokering is a fascinating field that can be filled with many personal as well as monetary rewards. But it takes hard work to get your service going. If you are uncomfortable in the role of salesperson, you probably won't make it—no matter how good a researcher you are.

If you like sales or team up with somebody who does, however, the market is out there. The business world wants solutions to their problems. They need thorough but concise access to information. That's why the business world needs you. You will have to convince them of that!

While there are a few large national services like my former company, Information on Demand, Inc., my experience has been that the marketplace has a psychological need to work face-to-face with a broker. So there is plenty of room for small, local information entrepreneurs.

Most brokers have a library/information service background, but I have consulted for many who come from other fields. The necessary traits are creative inquisitiveness, intelligence and the ability to work hard. These, coupled with the information in this book, will give you a good foundation and a fighting chance to be a success.

As a pioneer in the fee-based information industry, I know how frustrating the first couple of years can be. I wish there had been a book like this one when I was getting started to which I could have turned for practical help.

Best wishes for success in your exciting new endeavor.

—SUE RUGGE
THE RUGGE GROUP

Acknowledgments

So many different people and companies have contributed to the writing of this book that it may not be possible to personally thank them all. But in an effort to publicly recognize these folks, thanks to: the American Society of Hospital Pharmacists, Biosciences Information Service, Jacqueline Campbell, Ph.D., Chemical Abstracts Service, DIALOG Information Services, Inc., Disclosure, Chris Dobson, manager of the library at INFOMART, Dun's Marketing Services, Paul & Sarah Edwards of Here's How, Terence Fitzpatrick, Garland Publishing, Inc., Alfred Glossbrenner, J. Norman Goode, Bill Grout, agent extraordinaire, Information Access Company, Melissa Kirkpatrick of Cassandra Associates, Arthur D. Little Decision Resources, Ed Marsh, Ph.D., of Alabama A & M, Mead Data Central (Lexis/Nexis/Medis), Multnomah County Library, NewsNet, Packaged Facts, Predicasts, Sue Rugge of The Rugge Group, Bob Sherman of C.A.R.O.L., Source Telecomputing Corporation (The Source), St. Martin's Press, Telebase Systems, Inc. (EasyNet), VM Personal Computing, VU/TEXT Information Services, Inc., and LM Warren, Chris Wesselman of Research One.

Introduction

Welcome to the Information Age. You know it's the Information Age because that's what it says in the newspapers and magazines and what they say on radio and television. You confront it every time you sort through the ever-growing stack of unsolicited mail that comes to your door, or you try to remember where it was you saw that magazine article on a new way to fertilize roses.

People may tell you, "Information is power!" But information is just a mess of paper on your desk until you need it (assuming you even have the information in the first place). A more appropriate motto for the Information Age was given by John Naisbitt, author of the book *Megatrends*, "We are drowning in information but starved for knowledge." On the other hand, as Albert Einstein observed, "All the knowledge in the world is not wisdom."

The information problem many people face today is not a lack of information. The problem is simply too much information for any one person to possess all that is necessary for today's complex and changing environment. What is needed is information management that results, at a very basic level, in being able to find a given piece of information when it is needed without having to spend too much time worrying about it the rest of the time. That ability may be what Naisbitt was thinking of as "knowledge." Your ability to manage information will be crucial to your success, whether you are an employee of a major corporation, an entrepreneur, a student or an unemployed person (either by choice or circumstance).

The information professional offers knowledge through the management of information. The information professional has the talent and ability to take advantage of the latest in information technology while using traditional information management and retrieval skills. The information professional can help a client not only identify what information is required, but also help find it, interpret it and decide how to use it. The information professional might be on the staff of a local public library, the manager of a private library in a major corporation, or the director of an academic library at a major university. Sometimes the information professional is an independent entrepreneur—an *information broker*.

In truth, information professionals have been around for a long time; they are not a by-product of computer database services. The need to manage printed information has long demanded specialists to catalog, store, retrieve and analyze it. Even Alexander the Great had an information problem. However, the tremendous increase in the amount of information available, the many new technologies that allow it to be gathered, analyzed and used in new ways, and the importance of information to decision-makers is helping give the information professional a critical role in any decision-making process.

Fee-based information services (an unwieldy but descriptive phrase) are developing from a number of sources. Some public, academic and special libraries offer research services for a fee, either to the general public or just a specific group. Some corporate information centers are available to perform research for outside interests. A handful of major information services offer everything from online research to document delivery to specialized report generation. And in spare bedrooms, kitchens and small offices across the country, individual information entrepreneurs are taking advantage of today's technology to offer services not previously within the reach of small business.

It would be easy to imagine that the future of information brokering rests in the hands of the major services like FIND/SVP, Information on Demand, and The Information Store. These companies do appear to be doing quite well. A story broadcast on CNN in August of 1987 reported revenues for FIND/SVP of $10 million per year (not including, evidently, their very active report-publishing activities) with those revenues increasing at about 25 percent per year. With 1,100 clients nationwide submitting 7,000 queries per month, FIND/SVP has what CNN called a "major growth opportunity."

While FIND/SVP most certainly has a future in the information industry, there is ample room for new players, both those with dreams of an organization the size of FIND/SVP and those who are content to operate a small business from their home. Sue Rugge, founder of Information on Demand, agrees that much of the future of information brokering is as a cottage industry. While a small number of large firms may dominate the information industry, a significant market share is available to the individual information entrepreneur.

It is to these pilot fish of the information industry that *Information for Sale: How to Start and Operate Your Own Data Research Service* is directed. Whether you are now a librarian (or studying to be one), a subject specialist with an interest in having your own business, or an information junkie looking for a way to get your computer to pay for itself, this book can help you understand the business side of information brokering. You will be introduced to the tools of information brokering, walked through the establishment and operation of an information service, shown a sample search from the initial request to the final result, warned about legal pitfalls, brought up-to-date on the latest technological advances affecting the information industry, and referred to other valuable resources you can use in planning and operating your information brokering service.

Chapter Summary

Chapter 1 will introduce the role of the information broker as a free-lance information professional and define the general market for and function of the information broker.

Chapter 2 will outline basic areas of starting an information brokering service. It will examine research itself as an academic and business discipline and will discuss the "value added" nature of information brokering. This chapter will consider the type of equipment and other resources essential to the business and discuss the operation of a small business, including the preparation and use of a business plan.

Marketing is the most important aspect of running a successful information brokering service (or any other small business, for that matter), and Chapter 3 will examine marketing in general and look at how marketing this service presents special challenges. The chapter provides samples of promotional materials and the experiences of other information brokers.

It is difficult to place a specific value on information and, it is also difficult to place a price on the services of an information broker. Chapter 4 will discuss the pricing of a service both as a financial exercise (fixed vs. variable costs, cash flow, etc.) and as it specifically applies to information brokering. Other information professionals will share their pricing policies.

Chapter 5 examines the question of copyrights on the results of an online database search from the perspective of the information producer and the broker. Contracts, liability, and other legal considerations will also be reviewed. A sample contract and letter of agreement will be provided.

The pace of change is rapid in any technology-dominated field such as the information industry. CD-ROMs, gateway services, search software, full-text databases and other emerging technologies bringing change to the field will be discussed in Chapter 6.

With the help of Chris Dobson, manager of the library at INFOMART in Dallas, Texas, Chapter 7 will develop an online search to be used to generate a bibliography of articles a prospective information broker should read. Tips for more efficient searching also will be provided.

The experiences of two information brokers, Bob Sherman of C.A.R.O.L. (Computer-Assisted Research On Line) and Chris Wesselman of Research One, are the focus of Chapter 8. They will tell how they got started in the business and how they manage and market their services.

Resources, including online database services (such as DIALOG, Dow Jones News/Retrieval and others), gateway services (such as EasyNet), software (such as Pro-Search), professional organizations, books, periodicals and articles are the focus of Chapter 9. While not a comprehensive list, these resources will start a new information broker on the hunt for the right information resources.

How to Use This Book

You might be tempted to skip over parts of this book and only read those sections of particular interest to you at the present time. Please resist this temptation. The information in *Information for Sale: How to Start and Operate Your Own Data Research Service* is presented in a logical progression. Read through the book once and then use it as a continuing reference to review those portions that most interest you.

Most of all, don't make any assumptions about quick and easy money to be made in information brokering. As with any business venture, with the right kind of preparation and effort you can make a reasonable profit from it. And, as with any business venture, you can find yourself several months and many dollars later with only the ruins of what could have been your future.

The Information Age will be here for a long time to come, and the information broker will continue to be a major player in the field. Do you think you fit the requirements for an information broker? If you follow the guidance offered here (and the professional guidance you seek elsewhere), and if you work long enough and smart enough, you can be one of the many who succeed at and profit from information brokering. This book can be the first step towards your new career.

Welcome to the Information Age.

To Mark, who made it all possible,
and to Marianne and Matthew,
who made it all necessary.

—E.P.C.

To Sukie, She won't believe it,
but this couldn't have been written
without her.

—J.H.E.

Soli Deo Gloria

Chapter 1

Information and
the Information Broker

BEFORE BEGINNING A DETAILED EXAMINATION OF THE STEPS INVOLVED IN STARTING and operating an information brokering service, we'll look at some of the key components of the information industry, particularly as they relate to you and the kinds of decisions you'll have to make as an information broker.

The Role of Information

Some people suggest that when a person is unable to make a decision it is because that person simply does not have enough information. While there is a bit too much of the unlimited human potential movement in that generalization, having access to the right information at the right time often can ease the process of decision making. Unfortunately, most people don't recognize their indecision as an information need.

Everyone knows that information is available from the public library. In high school or college, you were assigned research papers that acquainted you with *The Reader's Guide to Periodical Literature, Books in Print* and other guides designed to help you get to the information that met your need. While you now may be prepared to write a good research paper, you may not have transferred that information-seeking talent to your current occupation.

Yet the same principles that apply in researching for a class composition apply to researching for business. And just as there are guides to help you find a magazine article on the development of Elizabethan drama, so there are guides to help you find the marketing plans and market share of the three largest suppliers of soft drinks in Europe. For many years, business people made seat-of-the-pants decisions because the information they needed was either not available, too expensive or too out-of-date to be useful. Today, current information often is available at a reasonable price.

So there is no longer any excuse for the business person who makes decisions without sufficient information. And yet the role of information is more than simply gaining access; you must gain access to the right information. Often a business person who recognizes an information need is unable to get the right information, not because it is unavailable, but because he asks the wrong questions. Wrong questions often are caused by addressing a symptom instead of a root problem, or by looking for a conclusion instead of information.

Information is not a precise science. As you will see (or may already see), many factors can make a bit of information more or less accurate, a source of information more or less useful, or the decisions based on that information more or less wise. Even if you know you have an information problem and you are able to get the information you need, you must still be able to interpret the information accurately and apply it to your situation. Having the right information is not the same as knowing what to do with it. Corporate raider T. Boone Pickens is reported to spend thousands of dollars each month on information. It's said that if someone in the oil business sneezes, Pickens knows about it quickly enough to say, "God bless you." You could have that same information, just as quickly. But would you know what to do with it if you had it?

The problem of information now may seem too complex for you. You might yearn for a simpler solution to your information needs. Someday you may be able to turn on a computer and ask, "Should I attempt a hostile takeover of Humongous Industries?" and get a yes or no answer. However, by that time you should also be able to get in your car and say, "Take me to Mother's." In other words, it's nothing to stay up nights waiting for.

Another option is available to you, however. You can hire an information specialist to help you identify your information need, define the right questions and identify the sources most likely to have the best answers, ask those questions and get those answers, analyze the information, recommend decisions based on it, and help you keep it handy once you get it. That person might be a corporate librarian (if your company is large enough and the librarian has the time and inclination and resources to help) or he or she might be an independent consultant—an information broker.

The Information Broker

So, in essence, the information broker is an independent information specialist who can help people who have an information need, meet that need, and make full use of that information. It might help to further define information brokering by listing some of the services an information broker might offer:

- Abstracting
- Analyzing information

- Assisting in grant preparation
- Bibliography collecting
- Cataloging
- Computer software design
- Consulting
- Current awareness
- Custom information services
- Directory compilation
- Document collection and delivery
- Editing
- Education and training
- Identifying experts
- Indexing
- Industry overviews
- Instant education
- Library management
- Library development
- Literature searching
- Manual searching
- Market research
- Needs assessment
- Online searching
- Publishing
- Purchasing reports
- Records management
- Seminars
- Specific subject updates
- Systems design
- Thesaurus construction
- Verifying facts

This is by no means an exhaustive list. It even might not include an area you've already identified as appropriate for your skills and interests. At one time, it might have been enough for the information broker to offer access to computer-assisted research techniques. It was a new technology with a strange set of rules and information brokers could easily claim to be the wizards of this new magic kingdom. However, the public awareness and acceptance of this new technology is growing (thanks in large part to aggressive marketing by the information services) and simply having access to an online service is no longer the ticket it once was.

This evolutionary development will change the services provided by information brokers, as well. When the service provided by an information broker mostly consists of accessing and transmitting information, it is easy for the client to believe that what she is paying for is information. In one sense, that may be true; many information brokers pass through the online and other information costs to the client (more on that in Chapter 6). But what is really being paid for is the expertise and effort of the information broker in preparing and conducting the search. This distinction becomes particularly important when a search turns up little or no information. Sometimes this is good (in searching for patent or trademark information) and sometimes it is bad (when searching for information on a privately held corporation). But in either case, a service has been performed and payment earned.

In describing an information broker it is also helpful to examine the distinctions between generalists and specialists. A generalist might research kumquats today, the cost of kites tomorrow, and Carole King the day after—or all three at once. A specialist is geared to one subject area such as economics or, even more specialized, global economics and its effect on the relationship of banks and Third World countries. In practice, the generalist information broker tends to search the more general databases, looking to find answers to broad questions. Clients with information needs in highly complex subject areas will tend to patronize information brokers who specialize in those areas. In Chapter 8, you'll meet a generalist, Bob Sherman, and a specialist, Chris Wesselman. Despite Bob's success, most experts today recommend specialization.

An important question for you is, "Do I have what it takes to be a successful information broker?" Throughout this book, you'll be asked to review your skills, interests and goals to answer that question. Right now, it might be helpful to look at qualities found in successful searchers. Speaking to the Seventh Annual Data Training Conference (December 1986), Jacqueline Campbell, Ph.D., discussed online database searching. As a part of her presentation, she looked at the "Qualities of Successful Searchers." She included the following qualities:

Innate Characteristics	Acquired Characteristics
Logical, analytical mind	Information skills
Communication skills	Knowledge of system vendors
Enthusiasm and curiosity	Knowledge of databases
Self-confidence	Typing skills
Decision making	Subject expertise

Do you have these innate characteristics of a successful searcher? Have you acquired any of the necessary characteristics (or are you willing to spend the time and effort to acquire them)? Take a little time to consider these questions before you begin your career as an information broker.

The Information Broker's Client

If you're having trouble seeing how a business person might need the services of an information broker, consider the following example offered by Terence Fitzpatrick:

I am a consulting engineer in private practice. I specialize in helping clients to identify and control risks, especially fire. One of my clients manufactures spray-painting and powder-coating equipment. They were working on some new electrostatic technology, utilizing high dc voltages (100,000 and up) and high-speed rotary atomizers (to 100,000 rpm). Their internal product safety consultant was concerned about special hazards posed by the latest advances. He advised his employer to seek approval from testing agencies (Underwriter's Labs and Factory Mutual) for "intrinsically safe" equipment. The marketing people, responding to the competition, didn't want to take the time. The National Fire Code requires "approved" equipment, but none of these devices at this time are approved (Catch-22). Industry is pushing the stuff, especially the auto industry. I needed some case histories of losses to support my paper, so I turned to DIALOG. I found numerous articles in numerous journals describing not just the fears of others, but specific details about actual fire incidents. What I didn't find was almost as interesting! Although I knew personally of several severe incidents in the U. S., almost all the articles I came up with were foreign! One of them was from Poland (closed society and all that), detailing their experience and requirements. One highly technical article was from a German publication, and was written by a former employee of my client's company! He about passed out! The client was so impressed, that he asked me to present my paper to his National Fire Code committee on spray application of flammable liquids.

Need another example? An attorney familiar with online database research tells with glee of a colleague who consulted him about a particularly difficult case. It seems the opposition had secured the services of an expert witness who was prepared to offer some very damaging testimony. This attorney suggested an online search to find out what this expert witness had published on the subject, hoping perhaps to uncover a contradiction to his current testimony. When a search turned up no record of anything on this topic published by the expert, the attorney was puzzled. He continued his search, looking for background information on the expert witness, and finally, in desperation (for his display of his much-loved online service was not going well), he searched Dissertation Abstracts for the thesis the expert had written. There was none. As it turned out, the expert witness was a fraud, having none of the credentials he had claimed. Don't you know the attorney enjoyed going to court and sharing the results of that online search?

Both of these examples highlight the power of online databases and they highlight the diverse applications of the kinds of information available online. Bob Sherman of C.A.R.O.L. has had as clients doctors, politicians, television producers, writers, companies that want corporate snooping, academic researchers and lawyers. Anyone who uses information (and who doesn't?) could use an information broker.

The Tools of the Trade

Online information services give access to tremendous amounts of information to anyone with a microcomputer and a modem. This is not to suggest the more traditional methods of research are no longer of any use. Online databases have limits. In general, only information published since the creation of a particular database is included in that database. The cost of going back and capturing previously published material is, apparently, too high. Exceptions do exist, such as the REMARC (REtrospective MAchine

Readable Cataloging) database which, when completed, will include works cataloged by the Library of Congress between 1897 and 1978. Information of interest only to a very small number of people (or only within a local area) traditionally is not found online because the potential market for that information is just not large enough to justify the cost of making it available.

So libraries, encyclopedia, microfilm and other traditional sources of information will continue to play a part in today's information age. A good information broker knows when to conduct a search online and when to get on the bus and go to the library. If a printed source of information is current enough for your needs, is indexed in a way that makes it useful and offers complete coverage of your subject matter, don't hesitate to use it. But if you need the most current information available, if traditional indexing methods won't help you find what you need and if you have to search many different sources, then an online search is indicated.

The history of the development of online database services has been told in other places (you'll find some of them noted in the bibliography). With the widespread use of electronic typesetting devices and the ever-decreasing cost of online electronic storage, there is little reason to expect the amount of information available online to do anything but continue to increase.

The information broker has a part in this burgeoning information marketplace. But it's a part that won't be had without hard and smart work. The information industry, as a whole, is driven by two primary factors. First is technology. You'll find that companies involved in the creation, distribution and analysis of information seem to be constantly chasing some new technology that is heralded as the major breakthrough they've all been waiting for. In many cases, the new technology does evolve into an important tool in the information industry, but sometimes it turns out to be just another fad that never really amounts to anything. Second is money. The major information services are interested in making a profit (no surprise here) and their product development will be directed in areas of interest to the people with the most money. Those people are not likely to be independent information brokers. So there's a challenge in using tools that are designed for another's hands.

The Future of Information Brokering

This may disappoint you, but *Information for Sale: How to Start and Operate Your Own Data Research Service* will make no attempt to specifically predict the future of information brokering. Too many predictions are made already and too many of them prove to be inaccurate. Consider the following:

Analysts at LINK Resources Corporation and International Data Corporation estimate a worldwide personal computer population at the end of 1983 of 13 million (10 million in the United States). The total is expected to reach 82 million by 1987. LINK forecasts that more than half of the low-end or ''home'' computers in the United States will be communications-ready by 1987, and there will be a somewhat lower percentage internationally. Nearly all of the 17 million ''general purpose'' personal computers, used primarily in business, will have communications capability by that time. Overall, a reasonable expectation is for 35 million potential online terminals to be in place in 1987, or roughly the total 1982 circulation of morning newspapers in the United States. (Used with permission from *Databasics: Your Guide to Online Business Information*. Copyright 1984 Garland Publishing, Inc. All rights reserved.)

In 1984, when this prediction was made, the future for microcomputers and for online database research was all blue sky and sunshine. The sudden downturn in sales of personal computers was generally unexpected. You must be cautious when making predictions.

Having said that, it is also important to say that unless the need for information stops increasing and, in fact, begins to decrease at a rapid rate, and until you can say to your personal computer, "Should I attempt that hostile takeover of Humongous Industries?" and get a valid answer, business will continue to need information specialists.

OK, you're convinced and you're ready to place your Yellow Pages listing as an information broker. Where do you start? Not coincidentally, that is the subject of Chapter 2.

Chapter 2

Getting Started

I T TAKES MORE THAN KNOWING HOW TO OPERATE A COMPUTER TO BE A SUCCESSFUL information broker. The ability to run a computer, or even to program it to do wonderful things, may be the least significant characteristic of a successful information broker.

Your success will depend on your knowledge, training, and abilities in several areas. First, you must be able to manage a small business—balance the books, send out the invoices (and dun the slow pays), manage the paperwork, maintain the office, etc. Second, you must be able to market your service aggressively. Third, you must be able to competently perform manual and online research in one or more subject areas. And fourth, you must maintain the perspective necessary to evaluate the progress of your business in relation to your business plan.

Marketing is probably the most important of these areas. It is the subject of Chapter 3 and will be discussed there in detail. The remaining areas are the subject of this chapter.

Before You Open the Doors

While this section of the book will occupy only a few pages, this part of your preparation will probably, and certainly should, take several months. The time you spend in preparation will save you headaches and heartaches later on. Do not shortchange this part of the process; this is a "pay now or pay later" proposition.

If you are now employed, you can begin preparations for your own information brokering business without quitting your current job. If you're still in school, you can begin making plans while still a student. Even if you don't have a job now, you must proceed carefully. If you rush to start your business, you will, in all probability, hurry its demise.

There are many places where you can learn the steps in starting a small business, and it would serve little purpose to duplicate those resources here. Books, courses and organizations can help you. One of the best and least expensive resources is the Small Business Administration (SBA). Too often, people think of the SBA only as a place to go for low-interest loans. In fact, the SBA has programs designed to help you avoid many of the pitfalls commonly encountered in starting and running a small business.

Two of these programs, SCORE (Service Corps of Retired Executives) and ACE (Active Corps of Executives) are worth a look. These are volunteer programs that offer counseling services to small businesses. ACE volunteers are still active in business while SCORE volunteers are retired—very often from their own businesses. There are some 400 chapters of SCORE or ACE in the United States, so there's probably one near you. SCORE also offers seminars on starting and running a business. These seminars cover determining how much money you need to start your business, marketing, bookkeeping, managing personnel and other areas. Both SCORE and ACE volunteers can help you whether you are just starting out, facing a problem in your existing business or ready to expand your business and just don't know how. For an SBA office near you, call the agency's toll-free number: (800) 368-5855.

The period of time before you're actually open for business may be one of the most important times in your business career. For that reason, you should take a look at some of the basic decisions and plans you will have to make as you begin your information brokering service. Again, this discussion will not replace the advice of an attorney or accountant, the assistance of a SCORE or ACE volunteer or the education of a college-level business management course.

The Successful Entrepreneur

This is a good place to stop and ask yourself a very important question: "Am I the kind of person who has what it takes to successfully start and manage a small business?" And just what kind of person makes a successful entrepreneur? A precise list is not possible, because someone out there is successful without conforming in any way to any list. However, we can identify a few character traits that seem common among successful entrepreneurs.

- They are careful and concerned about money.
- They often had jobs (paper routes, etc.) in their youth.
- They are competitive.
- They are willing to take risks.
- They have a lot of energy.
- They can set and pursue long-term goals.
- They persevere in problem-solving.
- They take the initiative.

- They make good use of available resources.
- They view money as a measure of accomplishment.

Perhaps you don't have each and every one of these traits. That doesn't mean you can't be a successful business person. But if you don't possess even a single one of them, you should reconsider your plans to have your own business. Of course, there are no guarantees either way.

Your Business Structure

The first question about your new business is, "What form of business is it going to be?" There are three general forms of business organization from which you can select the one that's right for you—sole proprietorships, partnerships, and corporations.

The comparative advantages and disadvantages of these three types of business organizations are always discussed in introductory business courses and you may already know what they are. If not, here's a brief summary:

Sole Proprietorship. This is the most common form of business organization for an information brokering service, and it offers several advantages. It is very simple and inexpensive to set up and you are unquestionably in charge of the operation of the business, and there aren't a lot of government forms required of a sole proprietorship. There are also disadvantages. As the sole proprietor, you alone are responsible for the support of your business. Should you become ill, the business would be endangered. The size of the business is more limited by your ability to keep it running. You are personally responsible for the debts and obligations of the business and it is easy to mix your business affairs with your personal affairs.

Partnership. A partnership is easy to form—you simply reach an agreement with your partner(s) to operate a business. You should, of course, have this agreement in writing and in detail. With a partnership, you have help in operating the business. You also have to split the profits (or share the loss) of the business with your partners. You are still personally liable for the debts and obligations of the partnership, whether you or a partner incurred the debt and whether that act was duly authorized. Should one partner die or wish to withdraw, especially in the absence of a written agreement, the business could become mired in a long legal battle.

Corporation. This is the most complex and costly form of business and should not be established without the help of an attorney. Stockholders are generally not personally liable for the debts and obligations of the corporation and the business takes on a life of its own, distinct from that of any of the founders, officers or stockholders. There is a lot less freedom of operation in a corporation and a lot more legal formalities and government forms. Corporate income can be taxed more heavily, as well.

In practice, most information brokering services probably begin as either sole proprietorships or partnerships and only later, when business conditions demand it, do they incorporate. The best business structure for you depends on a great many factors, and you should make this decision in consultation with your attorney and your accountant.

Once you have selected the structure for your business, you must begin to make plans for its operation. Not surprisingly, this process will result in what is known as a business plan.

The Business Plan

You may have heard a story about someone who started a business, did everything wrong and now is a huge success. What you don't hear are the thousands of stories about people who started a business, did everything wrong and declared bankruptcy. You can succeed without a good business plan. It just isn't very likely. The lack of good planning is a leading cause of business failure, but there's just no reason for you to fail for lack of planning.

People go into business for themselves for a number of reasons. They may want to be their own boss, set their own hours and go their own way. They may have dreams about the glory and glamour of running a business. You may share one or more of these dreams, but if you don't like working hard at making money, you may be disappointed in the reality of being an entrepreneur. In what may be one of the greatest understatements of all time, an article on franchising was entitled, ''Owning Your Own Business Not All Roses.''

All businesses have one thing in common—they exist to make money. Your business will use the money you start with and try to make more money with it: money to pay your operating costs, money to pay your salary and money to put back into the business. If you don't have the desire to make money, think twice about going into business for yourself. This is not to suggest that the acquisition of money should become your all-consuming purpose in life, but that earning money must be a driving force in your business.

Your business plan will help you develop a strategy for your business—how to get started and where to go from there. It will serve as a guide, reminding you of where you wanted to go and help you evaluate how you have gotten there. And it will give you an overview of your business that is important for you, and for the people you approach for help, to have. In developing your business plan, you will answer several basic questions:

- What business are you in?
- What services do you provide?
- What is the market for your services?
- How will you reach your target market?
- Who is your competition and how do you compare?
- What is the general outlook for your business?
- How will you keep tabs on your business?
- How much money do you need to start and operate your service?
- Where will you get the money you need?
- Where will you turn for help in starting your business?

In its booklet, *How to Develop a High-Technology Business Plan*, the accounting firm of Arthur Andersen & Co. notes:

> One of the most effective ways for an entrepreneur to attract investment capital is to develop a sound business plan and use that plan as a vehicle for generating investment interest. Though important, this is an ancillary use of the business plan, which should serve first as a means of charting and managing the growth of the business.

Your business plan should serve both purposes, in order of priority.

What Business Are You In?

What business are you in? Surely this is an easy question, right? It may seem so, but how you answer this question will have a great deal to do with your chances for success. Obviously, ''I'm in the information brokering business'' is not a sufficient answer to this question.

Consider a company that makes lamps. Perhaps the company thinks it is in the lamp business. If so, it will stress the structural soundness and functionality of its lamps. Or maybe it thinks it is in the illumination business. If so, it will stress the importance of good lighting and show how the proper use of its lamps contributes to good lighting. Or maybe it thinks it is in the mood business. If so, it will stress how the creative use of its lamps will set the proper mood in any room.

The type of advertising, the sales strategy, the packaging of the product, even the design work on new lamps would be influenced by the lamp company's decision about what business it was in. If it tried to sell ''lighting instruments'' to buyers interested in mood, using sales techniques suited for the illumination business, it wouldn't be around very long.

If you simply assume you are in the information brokering business, your business may not be around very long, either. Be more specific in your definition of your business. For instance, maybe you research new medicines and medical techniques used in other countries to help those people who are trying to get those medicines and techniques accepted here. Or maybe you help lawyers identify expert witnesses or help them find out what the other side's expert witness has said about a particular brand of lawnmower.

You're providing much more than access to a particular database. In fact, that aspect of your business may be inconsequential in defining what business you are in. *Define your business in terms your prospective clients will care about and understand.* Write down a short description of your business and see how it looks to you. Show it to others to see if it means anything to them. You might even show it to a few prospective clients to see what it means to them. Don't be afraid to change your statement. In fact, plan to review it at least once a year to make sure it is still accurate. If your business changes, change your statement.

What Services Do You Provide?

If you're having trouble deciding what business you are in, you can approach the problem from another direction. Start by deciding what services you are going to provide. From your list of services you should be able to construct a definition of your business. Chapter 1 listed some of the specific services that information brokers provide.

In developing your business plan, you should be trying to fill a business need that you have identified. Filling that need, in very general terms, is the service you will provide. You should use that as the basis for your business definition. But don't be too rigid. You must allow your definition to change as your business grows and changes.

Watch for patterns in your business. If you get a lot of requests for certain types of information, it might pay to develop a specific report on that topic and sell the report rather than repetitive research. Some large information brokering services do this and the development of desktop publishing will enable smaller firms to do the same. "On demand" publishing allows you to print out a report only when it is needed. In that way you can avoid the cost and inconvenience of maintaining a large inventory and also be sure the report you are sending out is as current as you can make it. You also can "publish" your report on floppy disk—save it in a format your client's computer and software can use. You can do this very inexpensively. Don't just download information from one database and think you're publishing. As you'll see in Chapter 5, copyright restrictions prevent your simply reselling the database.

Chris Dobson, manager of the library at INFOMART in Dallas, Texas, reports that her organization has gone into publishing. "We have come out with a bibliography on computer-assisted publishing, which includes desktop publishing and electronic publishing," she said.

> We started that as sort of self-preservation. We were getting so many questions on it, we put together a little bibliography we would hand out for free. The next month we added to it and the next month we added to it until it got to be 25 pages long. We decided that was too much to hand out for free, so we now charge for it. The first one covered April–November 1986. And then we did another one which covered November–December. It was just as big as the first one. We're selling those two and we're also selling a series now—it's basically a monthly subscription.

In the early days of online information, it was possible to be successful while providing information and services that people could get elsewhere, often for a lot less money. There are many free and low-cost sources of information, but most people didn't know they existed and these sources didn't do much to promote themselves. But now these sources are calling attention to themselves and other people are writing and talking about them. In addition to being a bit dishonest, trying to sell information that is available elsewhere for free is a bad business idea. Don't try to make a living doing things others are doing better or cheaper than you are. Find the things you can do better or cheaper than they can.

Pay attention to the services you are providing to see if they suggest other services you could provide. For instance, if a client asks you to research certain companies that are all involved in the leisure industry, you might suggest a general search of the business literature on changes in how Americans use their leisure time and its impact on businesses. Or you might suggest you find a published market report on the leisure industry. Don't just take the request, get the Securities and Exchange Commission or annual report information and walk away. Another assignment may be inside each job you get. Look for it.

If you haven't written your business statement yet, do so now. It will be a critical part of everything you do from here on.

What Is the Market for Your Service?

A more complete discussion of marketing can be found in Chapter 3, but by this point you should have some idea of who will buy what you will sell. If you live in a small town with only a handful of attorneys, it would be foolish to think you could successfully market computer–assisted legal research services. If you are in a major metropolitan area with a large number of attorneys working on their own or in small firms (probably without in-house online capabilities), you might find a ready market for computer-assisted legal research.

If you are thinking about specializing in a subject matter with which you are familiar, you probably already know many of the people who could benefit from your services. What you need is not just a short list of names, however. You should research the market to determine how many potential clients there are within the area you hope to serve. You should also project how many of them will use your service and how often.

Your local library will have directories to help you with some of this research. You can do your own primary research by approaching potential clients listed in the directory. Find out first–hand if members of your target market are interested in your service. Ask them to tell you if they think they could use you and how often. You can't always rely on what someone tells you, but you should be able to get some idea of the interest in your service. You'll also open some doors for later sales calls.

This is a point at which many people show their enthusiasm for their business. They make grand projections about their market penetration, the frequency of sales and the amount of money earned in each sale. You should do just the opposite. Assume a very low level of market penetration, lower than you think would be the least you could do. Assume a very low frequency of sales and a very low dollar value on each sale. This is no time to deceive yourself with rosy portrayals of the best of all possible worlds. If you can make it through the absolute worst times you can imagine, you just might make it through what will really happen to you. Who would have planned, for instance, for a prime interest rate of 20 percent or of gasoline prices at $2.00 per gallon? That could never happen, could it?

When you have completed your market analysis, you'll have some idea of how you fit into that marketplace, how you will be able to offer benefits your competitors can't or won't. Niche marketing is an important concept in this business. If you're going to serve physicians, try to decide which physicians you can best serve and most easily sell.

Are they older physicians who have been in practice (and out of school) a long time or younger physicians just starting their practice? Are they physicians in private practice or physicians working in public hospitals? "Every physician" in your area is probably too big of a target market. You must be able to tightly focus your marketing efforts.

How Will You Reach Your Target Market?

You've heard that if you build a better mousetrap, the world will beat a path to your door. What this rather naive tale of business success omits is the process by which the world hears about your mousetrap, becomes convinced it is indeed better, and locates your door. You may offer the widest possible range of information services at unbelievably low prices, but if nobody knows about you, that's exactly who will use your services.

Now that you've decided who will be interested in buying your services, you must decide how to let them know you're here. Again, Chapter 3 will provide a more comprehensive look at marketing, but in developing your business plan, you should discuss the means by which you will reach your target market. Your consideration of your promotional efforts should answer these questions:

- What is the message you want to send to your market?
- What are the best ways to get your message to that market?
- How much can you afford to spend (both time and money) on this effort?

Don't limit your consideration of promotion to ads or direct mail campaigns. Everything associated with your business will contribute to your image and to the message you are sending. This includes your letterhead and logo, the way you answer the telephone (or don't answer it when you're out), your attendance at business/social meetings, as well as your direct promotional efforts.

Who Is Your Competition and How Do You Compare?

An aspiring information broker once left a message on the Working From Home Forum on CompuServe, declaring that he had his computer, modem and DIALOG password and, since he was the only information broker in his city, he had the market sewn up. There was never another message from that individual. Perhaps he's been so busy serving his market that he hasn't had time to visit the Working From Home Forum again. Or perhaps he seriously misjudged his market and his competition.

You are not starting your business in a vacuum. If you are the first information broker in your city, you still have competition. There is the "old-fashioned" way of doing research—getting on the bus and going to the library. There is an even older method—doing without the information. Today, your competition could be from public or academic libraries or even from large companies trying to make money from their in-house research services. Don't just look under information brokers in the Yellow Pages (should you live in an enlightened city where such a listing is available) and think you have an exhaustive list of your competition.

Learning about your competition can even be a part of your market research. Find out how your prospective clients are meeting their information needs. Find out what they like and dislike about whatever method they use. You must not only know your competition but be able to distinguish your service from theirs. The more you know about your competition, the easier it will be to pursue the market niche you have chosen.

What Is the General Outlook for Your Business?

At present, there is little statistical data on the information brokering field and its prospects for the future. Most of what has been written is based on soft data—the expectations of people in the business and the outlook for the information industry as a whole. Fortunately, the projections for the information industry's continued growth are excellent.

The future of the information industry as a whole is a popular subject and you should have little trouble finding the latest guesses on this. But you should also look at the growth projections for your target market. If you're targeting small public relations firms in a five state region, what are the projections for this type of business in your area? If you can show a growth in the information industry and a growth in your target market, you should be able to project a similar growth in your business.

How Will You Keep Tabs on Your Business?

Consult with your accountant as you develop your budgeting and recordkeeping methods. Don't burden yourself by keeping more records than necessary, but have ready access to the financial information you need to make good business decisions. Your financial records should tell you:

- How much money you made.
- How you made that money.
- How much money you spent.
- What you bought with that money.
- How much money you have.
- How much money you owe.
- How much money you are owed.

You may also want other information, too. That is where your accountant can help you. At the very least, you should keep a cash journal that shows every dollar that comes in (and whence it came), every dollar that goes out (and whither it went) and every dollar that remains. It won't take a very complicated system to tell you that.

There are a few other devices you can use to keep tabs on your business. One such device is a cash flow journal. In simple terms, a cash flow journal can tell you how much cash you'll have at any given time. If you know that, then you'll know whether you need to arrange for additional cash to cover current expenses or whether you have excess cash on hand that you could be using to generate income. Over time, you'll also be able to compare your cash flow projections to your actual cash flow and, in this way, improve your ability to make those projections. Although this device, and others, may be too burdensome for a small information brokering service, you may not always be a small information brokering service. A sample cash flow estimate form is shown in Fig 2–1.

How Much Money Do You Need?

Another device essential to successful operation of a business is the budget. You have to know how much money you expect to make and how much money you expect to spend making it. Only then will you know whether becoming an information broker will make you money or cost you money.

Very simply, a budget is a projection of expected receipts and expenditures—your best guess at what your profit and loss statement is going to look like. While a budget really is just a guess, it should be the best-educated guess you can make. Your first budget guess will probably not be as well-educated as later ones, but you must make the guess anyway.

You can take at least two approaches to developing a budget. You can either estimate the amount of income you will produce and develop a budget of expenditures accordingly, or you can estimate the amount of money you will spend and devise the amount of income you will need to sustain that budget. In a new business, it is probably easier to use the second method, though many would argue that it would be more prudent to use the first. After all, it's more tempting to overestimate your income if you have a target level you want to reach.

If you use the second method, you will need to look at three items: fixed expenses, variable expenses and profit. Fixed expenses are those expenses that will not vary in proportion to how much business you have. Fixed expenses include office rent, utilities and the like. Variable expenses are those that vary in proportion to how much business you have. These include database access charges, printing, personnel costs (you may need another person to help out) and the like. Profit is what you want to put into your pocket.

In determining a figure for profit, don't just pick a figure that is close to what you think of as a good salary. You must also be able to buy for yourself items that an employee might be furnished, such as insurance. You should have some profit to put back into the business to finance future growth or see you through hard times. Also, if you put any of your own money into the business, you should pay yourself a decent return on that money. If you invested that money instead of opening your business, you'd earn a return on your investment. You instead chose to invest your money in your business. You should earn a return on that investment as well.

Once you have developed an expense budget, you must now develop an income budget sufficient to pay all of those expenses. Chapter 4 will discuss in detail how to

	JANUARY		FEBRUARY		MARCH		OCTOBER		NOVEMBER		DECEMBER		TOTAL	
	Estimate	Actual	Estimate	Actual	Estimate	Actual	Estimate	Actual	Estimate	Actual	Estimate	Actual	Estimate	Actual
CASH IN														
On Hand														
Sales														
A/R														
Other														
Other														
Total														
CASH OUT														
Supplies														
Online														
Wages														
Mktng.														
Rent														
Phone														
Taxes														
Other														
Other														
Total														
IN – OUT														
Net Cash														

Fig. 2-1. Sample cash flow estimate form.

determine what to charge for your services. In basic terms, you adjust your level of sales until you're selling enough to pay for the fixed and variable expenses and give yourself the necessary profit. Don't forget to adjust your variable expenses as you adjust your level of sales. Otherwise, you'll end up with a very inaccurate budget.

The other thing a budget will tell you is how much money you're going to need to operate your business. Again, this is no place to plan on unlimited success. Before you open your doors, you should have in hand enough money not only to open, but to operate for at least six months without a single dollar in income. Of course, you hope that doesn't happen, but you should be prepared in case it does.

Where Will You Get the Money?

Once you've gone through the budget-making process, estimating income low and expenses high, you may find you need more money to get into this business than you had thought. That is not unusual. And no matter how scrupulous you have been in preparing your budget, you'll discover expenses you left out. That is why it is so very important to be conservative in your estimates.

But you now know the amount of money it will take to get you started, to keep you operating during the first 6 to 12 months and to keep yourself alive during this time. It's more than you thought it was going to be. Your first reaction may be to go back to your budget and trim it down. If you find unnecessary expenses there, do remove them. But don't mislead yourself into believing that you'll get by with less money than your best estimates show you will need. No, you'll have to find the money somewhere.

If you've got the money in the bank, fine. Use it if you can afford to lose it. Remember to pay yourself a return on this additional investment. If you don't have the money, which is common, there are several places you can look for it.

You can borrow the money from family members, friends or acquaintances. While this money is often available at a very attractive interest rate, it sometimes brings you unwanted partners. It's very hard for a relative or friend to keep his nose out of your business once his money is in it. Use this route only with great care.

You can borrow the money from the bank. As an information broker, you won't have a lot of capital equipment to secure a bank loan and will probably have to secure it with personal assets. Again, don't use it unless you can afford to lose it. Consider the cost of personal bankruptcy if your business fails and you'll have some idea of how important it is to make your plans well.

You can borrow the money from another institutional source. People have started businesses with money advanced against their bank credit cards. You'll pay a very high rate of interest on the money, but it is a source. If you're a member of a credit union, you could talk with a representative about a loan. Life insurance companies will often loan you money against the paid-up value of a policy. Perhaps you've received a letter from a finance company asking you to come in and accept a loan. You could do that. Don't overlook any possible source of funds.

If you're turned down for a bank loan, you could talk to the SBA about a loan guarantee. The SBA ordinarily won't loan you the money, but they'll reduce the bank's risk and make you a more attractive borrower. Call your local SBA office for more information on this program.

You can look for a professional investor with some venture capital to invest in a new business. A few success stories about venture capital have probably raised expectations about the availability of this money beyond what is truly there. Also, the venture capitalist will want a major say in your business to protect his or her investment. This is probably not a good route for most information brokers, but if you can make it work, do so.

When you approach any of the above sources for money, you should be prepared to provide them with certain information, including

- Who you are.
- What kind of business you are starting.
- How much money you need.
- What you plan to do with that money.
- How you plan to pay the money back.
- Your business plan.
- Your personal financial situation.
- Why you are qualified to successfully start and operate this business.

And it wouldn't hurt your cause if you could produce a client or two, ready to buy your service.

Where Will *You* Turn For Help?

They are expensive and you may think you don't need them, but get yourself a good lawyer and a good accountant. It may seem like a lot of money, but they won't have to keep you out of too much trouble before they earn it.

Don't just let your fingers do the walking and select these professionals because you liked their ads. Shop around. Interview several candidates and make your selection carefully. You'll be paying for their time and effort and you have a right to have people you like and trust.

Find out if they have any experience with small businesses, with information businesses, with the kind of business you plan to have. Ask them about what they can do for you and what it will cost. Be specific. Make sure each of you is comfortable with the other. If you have to walk into a courtroom or an IRS audit next to this person, how will you feel?

You should expect different things from an attorney than you do from an accountant. An attorney can help you select the best form for your business and help you find out what permits, licenses and registrations you need. An attorney can help you anticipate and avoid legal problems and, when you encounter one, represent you effectively. Start out with a lawyer. Don't wait for a lawsuit to look for one.

An accountant also can help you choose the best form for your business as well as devise the best recordkeeping system for you. An accountant can help you interpret the financial information this system produces and help you plan the best tax situation for you and your business. The accountant, in short, will be your primary financial advisor.

We cannot over-state the importance of choosing competent professional help. It is so tempting to let this item slide on by, thinking you'll get to it later—except later is often too late. You're putting a lot of preparation, effort and money into getting your business started. Don't risk it all by overlooking this point.

It is in your best interest to take the time to prepare a well-thought out business plan, bring in the most qualified advisors, and create a solid foundation for your business. Once you're up and running, you won't have the time to keep up with yourself unless you've implemented the right kind of management systems. And if you wait until then to hire the professional help that every business needs, you'll have waited too long.

Your Business: Information Brokering

Those are the general points that apply to any business. There are some aspects that are peculiar to information brokering.

For instance, as an information broker, you might think you'll be spending your time finding answers to clearly defined questions. But research doesn't consist merely of finding the answers to questions. A successful information broker might spend as much time precisely defining a question as answering it. In business situations, an individual might feel the need for more information to decide something, but not know exactly the information needed or how to properly ask for it. If an information broker cannot work with that client to properly and completely define the information need (the question), then neither the client nor the information broker will be satisfied. The information broker will have lost a client and the client will still be unable to make an informed decision.

The importance of this process cannot be overemphasized, for if the question is not properly defined, then all of your research resources will be of no help. Don't assume that all persons in business have a real understanding of their information needs and will call you with well–defined questions that lend themselves to ready answers. You will have to be prepared to talk with the client at some length in order to accurately determine the question. If the account, and the problem, is big enough, then an in–person interview is advisable; otherwise, a phone call should do.

Once the question is properly defined, it is time for you to really go to work. Knowing what to ask for is the first part; knowing where to ask for it is the second. Information is available in two forms: primary information is information you generate or discover yourself (perhaps through a mail survey), while secondary information is information generated or discovered by another individual and published in a form available to you.

The second type of information is most often of interest to an information broker. Secondary information is available in two forms: the information itself (sometimes called *fulltext* when referring to articles or other published text) and *bibliographic references* to the information (i.e., where to find the fulltext and what is in it). Both forms are available by manual or computer search, and both have their uses.

You are already familiar with these two forms of information. When your favorite computer magazine arrives, you read through it, taking note of certain articles. You are searching through a full–text database and retrieving specific information of interest to you. If only for the purpose of writing a high school research paper, you have spent some time in the library with the *Reader's Guide to Periodical Literature* and/or *Books in Print*. These bibliographic reference works can guide you to specific articles or books on the topic you are researching without requiring you to read through every source that might deal with the subject.

The benefits and shortcomings of the two search methods should be obvious: Doing a full-text search manually would be an enormous task. Even if limited to only two weekly magazines over a three year period, you would have to read 312 magazines at, say, 120 pages each, for a total of 37,440 pages of information. You can see how quickly such a search could get out of hand. In a bibliographic search, you are depending on a third party to give you the essence of the information, and the interests and priorities of this third party may not be the same as yours. Fortunately, the advent of computer databases and searching has made the full-text search more manageable, and the long experience of those companies that produce the major bibliographic resources has enhanced their ability to accurately abstract the contents of an article or book.

The discussion so far has centered on text information, which comprises a significant portion of available data. However, a wealth of numeric data is also available, and this data may be of interest to your clients. Most numeric data is secondary, full-text data; that is, the numbers were generated through the efforts of a third party and are available in their entirety. Abstracting numeric data is difficult, though summarizing it is less so. It is also relatively easy to state concisely the contents of a record so that the searcher knows what is there and whether it is pertinent to the question.

Choosing a Specialty

Many early information brokers came from a library background. They turned their expertise, originally provided under the auspices of a public or university library, or developed within a large corporation, into a successful business for themselves. Many included their previous employers among their initial clients. Someone from a library background will have an advantage over someone from a business background or a computer background as far as research skills go. But information brokering is open to those without professional library experience if those individuals bring an expertise of another kind to the business.

If your only experience with research is writing themes in high school and/or college, you may have a tough time being a successful information broker. However, if you have expertise in a subject area or discipline, that can partially compensate for your lack of library experience. Through your work or course of study, you may have developed a high awareness of the information needs for a specific business: investment analysis, market research and planning, public relations, or some other field. Your understanding of the nature of this discipline and its special information needs and resources can give you a significant competitive advantage as an information broker.

If you have no library experience/training and have not specialized in any specific discipline to the point where you have developed real expertise in it, all is not lost. It is possible for a generalist to be a successful information broker. By choosing an area of concentration in which you yourself are interested and marketing your service vigorously, you can develop a service that might attract and be able to handle such unusual questions (offered by Bob Sherman of C.A.R.O.L.) as, ''Do chickens wear contact lenses and, if so, why?'' and, ''Does Bill Cosby have a doctorate and from where?'' You must realize, however, that your market will be more difficult to define, locate and reach than that of a specialist, and more of your time may initially be non-billable time, that is, time spent marketing and selling your service (rather than providing it) and gaining research skills. You must allow in your planning and budgeting sufficient time to build the clientele that will sustain your business.

Chris Dobson of INFOMART says, ''If your primary product is online database searching, specialize. It is impossible for one person to keep up with what databases are available in every field, much less know how to search them.'' As you become more familiar with the many online information sources, you'll come to appreciate her point, particularly once you see how quickly things change in this industry. When selecting your specialty, Dobson suggests you base your decision on your ''academic background and previous work experience, and on the types of businesses which will make up your target market.''

The Technology of Information Brokering

The field of information brokering is dependent on technology, and you may be wondering just what kind of equipment and software you'll need to be a successful information broker.

First, the moment you've all been waiting for—the computer. If you've held out this far in hopes of finding that the perfect computer will guarantee your success, you're going to leave disappointed. Almost any microcomputer will do. Some databases require specific software, thus restricting your choice of hardware; some restrict your choice of hardware directly, though most do not. You'll need a computer with a modem, communications software, the ability to capture data received via the modem, massage that data, save it, and print it out. This hardly limits your selection.

In buying a microcomputer, there are only a few simple instructions for you to follow. Most people buy a computer backwards. They become enchanted with a particular piece of hardware they've seen advertised on TV and go out and buy it. After getting it home and assembled, they try to figure out what they can do with it. The correct method is first to decide what you want the computer to do; second, to find software that will do that, and third, to buy a computer that runs that software. It may not be that easy for you, but at least you'll be coming at the task in the right way.

In talking about computers and databases, don't forget the wealth of non-computer resources still available. In fact, some information may not be available online. Your public library will be a good source of local community and business information. Sometimes all you have to do is call them on the phone and ask them for a piece of information, other times you must go get it for yourself. Also, all colleges and universities have libraries. Sometimes special libraries concentrate on a specific discipline—something to consider when making decisions about your area(s) of specialization. Large corporations have special reference material pertaining to their area of business, and oftentimes governmental agencies will operate specialized libraries (*e.g.,* a county law library, a state library on that state's history). Don't overlook these important resources by assuming that absolutely everything you need will be available online. Such is not the case. In using your library, do remember that the library staff is not your staff. Feel free to ask questions, but don't abuse their time. If you regularly need the assistance of a professional librarian, hire one.

At first, your clients may have questions you don't feel competent to research, at least not yet. Don't feel that you have to turn this business down or do an inadequate job of the search yourself. Neither approach is likely to make this client a repeat customer, and you will need many repeat customers to succeed. If you get a question you can't handle, consider accepting the assignment and then subcontracting the work to a competitor, whether another local information broker or a national search firm. Your client need never know that you did not do the search yourself (does it really matter?) and, if you went to a local competitor, maybe your competitor will come to you as you establish your area of expertise and your reputation.

At least one information broker suggests that anyone interested in getting into this line of work begin by marketing the services of another broker to see whether they can sell. It's possible to do this while also making a name for yourself and building a pool of clients. You can market the research service in your own company name while subcontracting the actual research to other brokers. The identity of the person sitting at the keyboard is not material here, and you are gaining valuable experience in nearly every other aspect of running an information service. If you later choose to pursue a career as an information broker and perform the searches yourself, your clients may never notice the change. In fact, if you hire people to do the actual online research, you may never find yourself sitting at the keyboard.

Chapter 3

Marketing

A S A PART OF HER WORK IN THE LIBRARY AT INFOMART, CHRIS DOBSON IS INVOLVED in marketing. At times, it might seem to her that all she does is marketing. But there must be no confusion about the importance of marketing, as she explains:

> No matter how good a researcher you are, if you can't sell, you won't make it as an information broker. And information is hard to sell. You either have to be there just when the customer has a question, or you have to spend lots of time educating the customer on the value of information and how he should be using it in his business, basically creating a need. As a result, you have to get your name and your business before the business public again and again. Too often, if you send out a flyer, the recipient thinks, "Gee, that might be handy someday," and has lost the flyer by the time "someday" arrives. In marketing, too, you have to specialize. Don't waste time and money trying to sell people who only need your services occasionally or don't recognize that they need them. Figure out who the heavy information users are that match your expertise and go after them.

Many people confuse marketing with advertising or selling. While advertising and selling are parts of marketing, marketing is more than just the combination of the two. Marketing includes:

- Defining your product or service;
- Identifying your most likely clients;
- Positioning your price and product in relation to other information options available to your clients;

- Making your product or service available to your clients; and
- Advertising and selling your product or service.

By examining each of these areas, you can build a marketing strategy best suited to your talents and your market.

Defining Your Product or Service

You will need to choose between being a specialized information service and a generalized one, based on your particular abilities, experience and interests. You also must consider your market when making this decision. Then, remembering what decision you made and why, you begin to construct your business and market your product or service.

In even a basic question such as selecting the database service(s) you will use, this decision is an important one. Generalists may be able to develop a good business using only the major, general interest databases, such as BRS or DIALOG, while specialists must sign with less well-known but more tightly focused services. Even the generalist, however occasionally, will have to turn to the more specialized databases as the major services continue to pursue the "end user" market.

Look around your community (or region, or state, or country, depending on how broadly you define the geographic limits of your market). What are the major activities now going on and planned for your market area? The area's chamber of commerce can provide basic statistical data on demographics and the economy, as well as projections of future development. The business departments of local or area colleges and universities often produce or host seminars and workshops on business trends and forecasting. These seminars are sometimes available commercially as well.

Buy and read business publications for your area. Most major metropolitan areas have a business newspaper or magazine, and almost every state does. These can provide raw data in the absence of an active or cooperative chamber of commerce. Of course, if you plan to specialize, get your hands on the professional or industry publications relating to your area of specialization. Watch carefully for discussions about future trends in your area or discipline. Information about yesterday's concerns is worth very little, even if it is available at the speed of light. Pay attention to what people expect to be taking place 6 months or 6 years from now. Shedding light on the future is an area in which information brokering could be most valuable and, perhaps, most readily accepted.

What Information Business Are You In?

As discussed in Chapter 2, each and every business must periodically ask itself a very basic question: "What business are we in?" You must not offer too pat an answer to this question. How you define your business will affect the way you see yourself and the way others see you. If you define it incorrectly, you may never match your product or service with its appropriate market. Remember the discussion about the lamp manufacturer? The same principles apply to you.

In a general sense you are in the information business, a business that is geared more towards response than initiative. That is, it usually responds to needs your clients articulate rather than to needs you perceive and pitch to the client. But you may have to work with the client at length to get that need articulated, or you may even have to carve out a market segment by identifying a new information need first and then selling clients on both the need and the service by which it can be met.

You may find that people in your target market are very unsure about their need for information. Business people often don't understand the role of information, the sources of information or the value of information. If you look for clients with ready-made questions, you may run into difficulty. Look for clients with problems. They are much more common. Show them how their problems are information problems and how you can help solve them. For example, instead of telling a university president about your access to Dow Jones News/Retrieval and DIALOG, you should explain how you can locate sources of funding for the programs that the university is planning to undertake.

This problem/solution approach to information brokering is a result of the growth of the information business. As noted, it once was sufficient for an information broker to provide access to the mysterious and wonderful world of online information. The clients were so thrilled to get the information they didn't care how hard it was to use. Today, clients expect something more. They want information presented in a useful manner so they can easily find the critical points and quickly make their decisions. They don't want to struggle through pages of output, looking for a central piece of information. This is the first step in distinguishing *information retrieval* from *information analysis*. It also is an important way in which you can add value to the information.

You also can distinguish your service by providing more than a bibliography of sources or abstracts of documents (in the case of text research). By using any of the numerous document delivery services—or doing it yourself if you live near a major library—and by taking advantage of the growing number of full-text databases, you can provide the original information sources. If you have the necessary subject expertise, you can then produce your own set of abstracts designed to answer the client's specific question. This also adds value and distinguishes you from a service that merely retrieves online information. It also adds more value than a client's personally performing the search.

These are just a few of the ways in which you can define the business you are in, beyond just "the information business." These decisions also will be important when you are pricing and selling your services.

Defining Your Most Likely Clients

Once you have defined clearly the business you are in, you have fairly well defined your product or service and partially defined your client base. As it would be impossible to adequately answer the question, "What business are you in?" without some idea of what clients there will be, you may think you already know the answer and can skip this part. Don't. You must fully understand what business you are in before you can identify your target market, and you must identify your target market before you can sell your service.

One way of looking at the potential market for your services is to examine the marketing strategies and methods of others in the information industry, including other brokers and the database publishers and vendors. Markets they have identified as key for their services might also be key markets for your service. This is particularly true of products and services aimed at the "end user" market, such as DIALOG's Business Connection. Target areas for this service would include mergers and acquisitions, financial analysis, strategic planning and competitive analysis. That's a very large market.

To look at marketing in a more specific example, suppose you have decided to target attorneys with your business, figuring that they have a high information need and an understanding of the cost and value of information (as they often do). You may look in the Yellow Pages of your phone book and decide that there are hundreds or thousands of attorneys in your area and each and every one of them is going to be your client. Would that it were so. Unfortunately, attorneys come in various shapes and sizes, with special packaging, interests and habits. Many of them never will be your clients.

Here's how to identify those attorneys who won't be your clients.

Suppose you are going to offer to search legal databases, social science databases, federal government regulations databases and professional publications databases for law firms. Most major firms will have in-house access to these databases, or will be receiving regular printed updates containing the same information. They may also have an in-house staff with the responsibility for researching questions for the attorneys and maintaining the in-house library. Offering to do something they can do quite well themselves is a very poor marketing decision in most cases. If you could search databases with which their staff may be unfamiliar, you might offer a desirable service at a competitive price. However, you might just give them an idea for a database to add to their in-house system.

At the other end is the small law office, often a one-person firm. This attorney might do business with a small circle of friends, work only in familiar areas of law, make a nice living, and have no desire to expand the business beyond this level. Such an attorney might use your service, but it will mean abandoning a comfortable way of doing business.

The same would be the case with a third type of non-client attorney: the veteran so used to one way of doing things that the advantages of a new way of researching are outweighed by the hassle of changing a long-held habit. While this may not really be the case, if the attorney believes it to be true, then his or her decisions will be made as if it were true.

Not all areas of an attorney's work require extensive research. Generally, a case on appeal requires more legal research than one at trial, where there is an emphasis on the determination of the facts of the case. And certain areas of law, such as the writing of a will, do not require extensive research.

The last type of attorney who is not a likely client would be one employed in-house with a major corporation. Having only one client—one that generally can give advance notice of its needs—this attorney does not suffer the competitive pressures of one in private practice. Such an individual would be difficult to convince of the need for your service.

Having pursued this line of reasoning this far, you may have defined your client base by process of elimination. You can get statistics on the number of attorneys in your market area and the percentages that work for major firms, for corporations, and in smaller offices. Working the percentages can give you the number of attorneys in offices of, say, five or fewer lawyers, and you might guess that at least one-half of those might be interested in expanding their business without increasing their workload.

While acknowledging the in-house availability of online searching at many of the larger firms, you should see marketing possibilities there, as well. You may find—as you discover the number and range of online services available, the complexity of many of the services and the variety of command languages in use—that it is all somewhat intimidating. Firms with in-house systems discover the same thing. They may use one service very frequently. They may subscribe to other services but not use them very often. Some services that would be useful to them they don't subscribe to at all. If you can make these services available to them, you'll have a client already well aware of the potential for online research.

This, then, is your potential market. If capturing a very small piece of it will give you a living wage, then you have a good idea. Otherwise, you ought to rethink your market area, your specialization or your whole venture.

Positioning Yourself

The next step is to realize that you are but one of several information alternatives. Your prospective clients have options other than using your service, even if no other information brokers are operating within your market area (a situation becoming less likely all the time). These options range from utilizing an in-house computer-assisted research system to doing without the information altogether. You should view yourself as competing against each of these alternatives, and plan your marketing strategy accordingly.

As with attorneys, businesses with in-house systems might not make good prospects, at least for searches on systems they use frequently. The situation will differ depending on your market area and specializations, but most of the time major corporations with in-house systems will use outside brokers when their service is too busy or when the necessary database isn't available through the in-house system. So don't completely write off large companies as clients, but use some discretion in predicting how, and how often, they might use you.

Here's a tip about marketing to large organizations with in-house online research capabilities. Don't approach the head of the organization with your marketing pitch. Somebody on the staff is responsible for information retrieval; you may threaten his job security by ''going over his head.'' Talk to the information specialist—the person most likely to make the decision to use an outside service and the person most familiar with the strengths and weaknesses of the in-house system. Be a friend, not a threat. You'll get more business.

Another information alternative available to your client is manual searching, either through an in-house library or through public and other outside libraries. This method has the advantages of appearing to be cheap and of having been used, with some success, for a great many years by a great many people. In fact, sometimes manual research is the correct method. Reliance on manual research will be a habit hard to break, particularly if your client has trouble seeing how much manual searching really costs.

There will always be those who think they can do without the kind of services you offer; they have always relied on their "gut feelings" and been successful, and they expect to continue to operate in this fashion. Maybe these are the same people who vote for a bond issue to fix an area dam only after a flood. Persistence may wear these folks down, but it may be only in their next business venture that they will come to you for help.

Given these three basic information alternatives, how does using the services of a competent information broker compare? For the major firms with an in-house system, you can offer your services when their staff is behind schedule, unable to tap into the necessary databases, or unfamiliar enough with those databases so that you can search them more efficiently. For the firms that use manual searching, you can demonstrate the actual cost of a manual search (hourly wage of searcher, plus loss of that person's time for use in other ways, plus expenses like mileage, parking, etc.) and show how computer searching is more thorough and accurate. For business people who would rather do without the information, you can demonstrate how access to information through a service such as yours can enable them to anticipate future business conditions and prepare for them. If a business manufactures a product using imported rubber, shouldn't that business be aware of developments in the synthetic rubber industry?

In thinking about how to motivate potential clients to try your service, view the situation from their perspective. You must understand what is important to them and present your service as something that will help them reach their goals. Remember, the best way to get people to do something you want them to do is to show them how it is in their own best interest. Telling them about your new computer, or the huge number of databases you can access, or showing them the neat graphics you can print out will accomplish nothing unless you can translate those features into a service that meets their perceived and/or real needs.

Pricing Your Product or Service

If there are other information brokers in your area, you must price your services in relation to them—though not necessarily the same as nor lower than. For a lengthier discussion of pricing, see Chapter 4; here pricing will be discussed only as it affects marketing. While there is a good chance that there will be other information brokers operating within your market, probably none will offer the same service in the same way to the same target market. This is what gives you some flexibility in pricing your service.

There are several ways to differentiate your service. For example:

- You may offer document delivery as a supplement to your research service,
- You may hand deliver the results of the search in a very short time,
- You may offer free consultations to help the client define the question, or
- You may just search and report and nothing else.

What you offer, and what your competition offers, will help you choose how to price your service. Remember, it is not just what you offer, but how the client perceives what you offer, that determines the value of your service. This is a subjective process all the way around.

Here are a few things to consider when setting your prices:

- How much is it going to cost you to provide the service?
- How much do you want to make?
- How much is your competition charging?
- How critical is this information to your potential clients?

Answering these questions will give you the basis for making good pricing decisions.

A basic pricing practice is to use fixed and variable costs to compute how many units (hours? searches?) need to be sold at what price to generate the desired dollar return. In other words, you may need 50 clients each using you 24 times per year at $50/hour plus expenses, or 20 clients each using you 6 times per year at $200/hour plus expenses, to make the business a success. There is no way for this book to tell you which one is best. You must make the judgement based on your ability to generate the necessary amount of business at the necessary price, and choose your course accordingly.

If, in looking at your options, you decide that the competitive situation is such that $200/hour is not going to attract the 20 clients 6 times a year, and $50/hour will attract more than the 50 clients 24 times a year (and the market will sustain that level of use), then the choice is obvious. If both seem possible, then the choice can be made on the basis of how you would like to work, for whom, and how much. But, rest assured, there is going to be a connection between your fees and your market share. By looking at several different plans encompassing several different pricing structures, you can make some reasonable decisions about how to price your product or service.

Making Your Product or Service Available

Deciding how you make your product or service available to your clients may seem to be a rather unimportant consideration, but it is an integral part of the marketing process. You are offering your services as an alternative to your client performing the research herself. In performing the research, your client gets instant gratification of her information need. While you might emphasize the speed of your service, it will be slower than instant. So how, and how quickly, you deliver the results is an important point.

You may have noticed the consistent use of the phrase "product or service." This has been intentional. While in a very real sense you are providing a service—the researching of a clearly defined question to meet a clearly defined information need—you also deliver a product—the report containing the results of your search. This product can be as simple as a direct printout of your search and its results (be careful of copyrights) or as complex as a full report with a summary, the information, and your conclusion.

How your product looks will be, in part, determined by your market(s), your subject(s) of specialization, and your pricing strategy. If a generalist, you may simply want to provide the unadorned results of the search, cleaned up to remove extraneous data and repackaged to comply with copyright restrictions. If, however, you are offering this service in an area in which you have some expertise, you may want to offer a summary and analysis of the results of the search as well. Rely on your instincts here, and take a look at what your competitors offer and why they offer it.

Also, consider how you will actually transmit reports to your clients. You will probably find that having a number of options is best. Certainly, where time is not a factor, the post office can deliver a document across town or across the country. If speed is more important (and, since people are procrastinators at heart, it will be), a local courier service or national air delivery service (even the post office) can provide fairly quick delivery. It is also possible to use facsimile transmission—sending a photocopy by phone.

This last method might give you another idea: send the report electronically, computer to computer. Electronic mail services allow you to send messages directly to another subscriber to the system, or have it printed and mailed to a non-subscriber. This option may be useful, particularly when the client subscribes to such a system. Yet one more option should become more and more possible—sending a report directly from your computer to the client's computer. With today's more sophisticated communications software, you can even do this at night when system use and long-distance rates are lower. Sending a compatible floppy disk will do the same thing.

Computers are finding their way into a great many places where people don't know how to use them. The fact that your client chooses to use an outside research service doesn't mean there's no microcomputer in the office. With a little help from you (for a fee, of course), your client might even be able to place orders online.

The way you physically present and deliver your product to your client may enhance greatly your appearance as an effective, efficient professional, capable of keeping the promises made in the heat of the sales pitch. How good your product looks will have almost as much to do with your success as how good your product really is. Take the time and make the effort so your product will look professional.

Marketing from the Client's Perspective

If you are to take full advantage of your marketing efforts, you must be ready when the potential client calls and asks you to come to her office for an interview. You must be able to anticipate the questions she will ask and be ready to answer them quickly and succinctly. In his excellent book, *How to Look It Up Online* (St. Martin's Press, Copyright 1987, Alfred Glossbrenner includes a section on "How to Choose an Information Broker." He suggests the following questions be used in evaluating an information broker:

- Are you *simpatico*?
- Does the individual plan to do a pre-search interview?
- What research resources will the individual use?

- Does the individual have an area of special expertise?
- Which databases do they plan to search and what other steps will they take?
- What exactly will you receive?
- What will it cost?
- Is confidentiality likely to be a problem?
- What formal training and work experience have they had?
- Does the individual have any references?

No one prospective client will ask you all of these questions and most will ask you ones not on the list, but it is a good idea to be prepared for these types of questions. Here's a quick review of the questions and how you might go about developing your response.

Are you *simpatico*? You certainly wouldn't choose a doctor or a lawyer unless you felt you could trust him. You can't easily define this, but you know it when you experience it. So will your client. If your client doesn't like you, he won't use you.

Does the individual plan to do a pre-search interview? Of course you do. You couldn't possibly attempt a search without one. If you don't plan to do pre-search interviews, don't plan to be an information broker.

What research resources will the individual use? Your client will be familiar with many of the sources of information for her profession and she will expect you to be familiar with them, as well. An attorney would not hire you to do legal research unless you have access to either WESTLAW or LEXIS, and know how to use them. You can't bluff your way through this one. If you can't access the sources your client needs, tell her and recommend another course of action (or another broker).

Does the individual have an area of special expertise? If your client needs a very specialized search and you are a generalist, you should decline the assignment. If you've never used Chemical Abstracts and didn't do well in chemistry in high school, don't try to market to chemists. Also, if you're a specialist in mergers and acquisitions research and someone asks you to do a very complex medical search, you might not be able to do a good job for him. Rather than do a bad job, decline (or, as discussed in Chapter 2, subcontract the work to another broker).

Which databases do they plan to search and what other steps will they take? This deals with your thoroughness and your thoroughness will depend on the needs of the client and how much she is willing to pay. It is also another way she can find out whether you are familiar with the major resources of her subject area. This would be the point at which you also discuss other research options, such as manual research.

What exactly will you receive? The product you place in your client's hand will be the basis for her evaluation of your performance. You must make sure she knows what to expect and you must know what she expects. At a minimum, you should provide a clean, legible report. You might provide additional services, such as highlighting key parts of the report, providing photocopies of the appropriate articles rather than just the abstracts, etc.

What will it cost? Estimating is not easy, but your client won't want to turn you loose online without some means of controlling the cost. Not only should you be able to state your fees, but you should also be able to offer a reasonable estimate of the costs of the search and a process by which your client can control those costs.

Is confidentiality likely to be a problem? It had best not be. If your client's interest is in a sensitive area (perhaps she is an attorney representing a major client who is interested in acquiring a local company), she should have every assurance that you will keep the subject and results of your search confidential. You can't compromise; you must be able to assure your client of complete confidentiality.

What formal training and work experience have they had? Your client will expect you to understand her questions and be able to find and understand the answers. You don't have to be a lawyer to do legal research effectively, but you do have to have more than a passing acquaintance with the law.

Does the individual have any references? Do not offer any of your clients' names as references without first getting their permission to do so. Confidentiality should be a consideration. It is reasonable for your client to ask for references, but you should be cautious about choosing the references you use. Don't embarrass a client by giving their name as a reference to a major competitor. Of course, if you're just starting out, you don't have any clients to act as references. Since dependability and confidentiality are keys in this business, you might ask some close business associates to vouch for you in those areas.

Advertising and Selling Your Product or Service

Now to the consideration of advertising and selling your product or service. The volumes available to teach you how to do this won't be duplicated here. However, some considerations are of special interest to information brokers and should be examined briefly.

Information services have used a variety of advertising methods:

- Sales calls
- Attending conferences and meetings
- Professional journal advertisements
- Yellow Pages ads
- Newspaper ads
- Radio ads
- Direct mail
- Word of mouth

Making decisions about where and how to advertise is a function of your market and your potential clients. It is not enough merely to announce that you are open for business and then sit back and wait for success. You have a very specific, often unfamiliar product or service, and if you buy some of those little tombstone ads in the local paper, they may serve only their nominal purpose for your business. You've gone to a great deal of trouble to define your client profile. Use it in deciding how to best reach your potential clients.

While you may get some sales directly from your ads and/or your reputation, most of your early sales will come as a result of direct contact—a person-to-person sales call, or at the very least, a phone solicitation. So prepare your advertising accordingly. If you use direct mail, ask the reader to call for more information, or to send in a card for a free "information needs analysis," or booklet. To the business person with a limited understanding of what you can offer, a print ad will not readily communicate the essence of your product's value.

In advertising, remember to couch your product or service in terms of what it can do for potential clients. Listing the databases to which you have access will be of little interest to anyone except your competition. If you can offer "instant education" to someone needing to learn a lot about a product, discipline, country or individual in a short time, say so. If you can provide complete demographic data on any city in the U.S. and provide a marketing strategy to someone who is considering opening a new market, say so. Whatever it is, specifically, that you can offer your client that no one else can offer, say so.

Of course, if you are dealing with a specific professional or business market, you should consider advertising in the publications that cater to that market. This may not generate sales directly, but it will put your name in front of your prospects so that when they get a letter from you (maybe one you send to all who subscribe to that publication), it will not be the first time they have heard of you. This kind of reinforcement advertising can help tremendously, and by buying the ad, you may even make the publisher more cooperative when it comes time for you to rent their mailing list or ask that an article be written about your service.

Word of Mouth

One of the most effective advertising techniques for small service firms is word of mouth, especially in a local market. Satisfied clients can work wonders for you, and you should encourage them to recommend you to others. But don't overlook one of the most important mouths—yours. You offer a unique and interesting service. Tell people about it. Speak at a luncheon for a local service club. Offer to write an article about information and database research for the local chamber of commerce magazine/newsletter. Attend the meetings of organizations to which your potential clients belong, and carry a handful of business cards and brochures with you. Publicity can be free, and the contacts you develop can be the cornerstone of a successful information brokering business.

Your Brochure

A brochure is essential in marketing. When it is well-designed and well-written, it will be an important part of your marketing effort. It can cover the pertinent information your potential client is hungry to know. It can be a concise, specific compilation of how you can fill your client's wants and needs. It can be the thing that makes the purchase decision possible. Doesn't that sound as if it's worth about a quarter each?

What do you want in a brochure? To answer that question, start collecting brochures of other businesses and free-lancers of all callings. Many brochures will use an 8.5 × 11-inch sheet of paper with a single fold, making the finished size 5.5 × 8.5 inches. Others will use that same sheet with two folds so that it will fit into a standard business-size envelope.

Decide on the format you like. Look at the art in the brochures you've collected. Notice how the text is laid out on each page. How does the front panel look? Is the back of the folded brochure a self-mailer (that is, has it a return address and space to put in a potential client's address)? What about the typeface—is it modern, crisp, fancy, simple? Identify the elements in these brochures that you find appealing (and unappealing) and decide how these elements can be applied to your marketing brochure.

Then take a piece of paper of the appropriate size and fold it as you want it. On the front panel, sketch your cover. If you have not yet designed a logo, this is a good time to do so. You should also select a motto, and develop a distinctive letterhead so that your company has a distinct visual identity. Establish your identity on the front cover. The back cover, if the brochure is to be a self-mailer (which can save you money on envelopes), should include your return address. Or, if you feel you need more space for your text, you can work in a reply card as a part of the back cover. Perforations will make it easy for the addressee to detach the card and mail it back to you "for more information."

Now, you still have two inside panels, and perhaps part of a third, for your message. What should you say? If it's hard to blow your own horn, pretend you are writing this for your best friend or favorite sibling. Think of it as selling a product: be objective yet creative in describing the advantages of your product. Answer these questions:

- What are the benefits to your client of using an information broker?
- What could your client lose by failing to use your services?
- How can you save your client money?
- What specific services can you offer?
- Can anyone testify as to your expertise?
- What credentials do you and your staff have to offer?

Granted, research by computer is an abstract concept, and it will be difficult at first to think in emotional, compelling terms about information brokering. But put your enthusiasm into words. Use strong action verbs—no quibbling! Use modifiers such as fast, efficient, professional. Be selective and emphasize your most important qualities. Keep it believable by believing in yourself.

When listing your services, be sure to define them; this is not the place for jargon and buzzwords. Say things like, "For those who need to know now, our instant education service offers the decision-making information you need to know!" If your experience or list of satisfied clients is still pretty brief, don't despair. Talk about the people you'd like to be serving: "Data research for the not-for-profit community," for example. List the sort of jobs you'd like to be doing in the same terms. Say what you are capable of doing, even if you haven't done it yet. A few cautions: Don't name a former client or even quote from praising letters without permission. Don't list a lot of specific fees, either; you may need to adjust them. When that happens, your thousands of expensive brochures will be obsolete. If you feel you must mention your fees, include a range of fees instead.

Listing specific databases may not mean much to the reader unfamiliar with online research; or if the reader does know about a database, one that he considers essential, it might be one you decided not to list. If you're going to include a list, make it a partial list, and say that it is incomplete. Most of all, don't make guarantees you can't keep. Be positive, even aggressive, but don't overreach.

Take your sketch, rough copy and ideas to a graphic artist or a printer with design and layout capabilities. The total cost for 500 copies of a simple brochure (one color of ink and no photographs) will run $200 to $300 on average. If you are not happy with your artwork, consider hiring a professional graphic artist. This will cost a little more money, but an effective brochure is well worth it. A graphic artist can send you to the printer with "camera ready" artwork and even make suggestions about paper selection, color, and other features.

Your completed brochure is a powerful marketing tool. Think of it as an oversized business card. Leave one after every meeting, after every interview. Whenever you meet a potential client, follow up the acquaintance with a letter and a brochure. Try to send out several each week to potential clients you have identified through research or tips from friends. You may want to ask some clients (not relatives!) their reaction to your brochure before it goes into a second printing. Update it whenever you feel it's necessary, such as after some additional training or when you add a service. And don't forget to ask every prospective client, "Have you seen our brochure?"

A Sample Brochure

In preparation for this chapter, the authors distributed a letter asking that brokers send in copies of their marketing material for review. Packaged Facts submitted some very effective material that includes a clear, unmistakable logo used on every piece of paper the public sees. The logo is a paper clip enclosing the name of the company. When this package was sent, it was held together by a large, heavy, golden paper clip, continuing the theme. The small black-and-white ad (Fig. 3–1) has several good devices: the logo (of course), a reverse (white on black letters; notice that the type used is thick-bodied), a list of the main products featured, and the company's name and address. It also mentions, very clearly, what the services are. Too many small companies, when doing their own ads, forget to mention their product or service.

Their brochure is two-color, made to look much fancier by the use of screens and varying shades of the yellow-orange ink that is Packaged Facts' company color. Your printer can show you how screens can give two-color work more variety and depth.

Fig. 3-1. Black and white ad. Originally 3.5 × 5 inches, this ad could be run in magazines, newspapers and newsletters or printed on postcards for a quick direct-mail campaign.

The fold in the piece is a little off-center, so that the 15.5-inch width is divided into an 8-inch part and a 7.5-inch part. This creates a 1.5-inch underhang, inviting the reader to open the brochure. The underhang lists the company's intended markets (market professionals, ad agencies, etc.). If the reader fits one of the categories, he can't resist seeing what's inside.

The file-folder graphics inside are an image of business and efficiency. The list of services is specific. In all, it tells the reader what Packaged Facts can do for him.

Another marketing tool is the news release (Fig. 3-2). Notice the logo! The news release summarizes one of their reports, telling just enough to make an executive want to pay full price to see all 100 pages. Yellow paper carries out the company color scheme. The order brochure (for Consumer Market Studies, Fig. 3-3), again in black, yellow and white, briefly describes the available market reports and includes an order form on the back. Even the memo pads (Fig. 3-4) used in their office carry out this theme.

Two other examples of logos are in Fig. 3-5; these are simple, graphic ways to carry out the name of the company. Logos formed from the initials of a company are a popular theme. Just ask your lawyer (you do have one by now, don't you?) to check that your final design is not already registered by someone.

Figure 3-6 shows a nicely designed informational brochure from a library on its information services. Like the Packaged Facts brochure, this one uses a slightly off-center fold. It also used a line art picture of a computer on the front. Ask your printer if she has any books of "clip art," which may be where this was found. Inside, the large, bold head and small boxes make the information easy to read.

A very simple example of a do-it-yourself brochure is in Fig. 3-7. This is the inside

FOR IMMEDIATE RELEASE

press news from (packaged facts)

FROM:
Edward Weiss
PACKAGED FACTS INC.
274 Madison Ave.
New York, N.Y. 10016
(212) 532-5533

"ENERGY DRINKS" MARKET TO REACH
$385 MILLION BY 1992

Factors Propelling Growth:

1) The spin-off from the "fitness" trend

2) Increasing sales in non-traditional outlets
   like health food stores and health clubs

3) Companies expanding marketing efforts in
   institutional and and industrial outlets

New York, N.Y. -- The market for "energy drinks" -- i.e., isotonic and
hypertonic beverages -- is projected to grow from its current level of
$250 million to $385 million by 1992, according to a newly published study
by Packaged Facts, the New York research company.

The study pinpoints three major factors as propelling market growth: 1)
the spin-off from the fitness trend, 2) increasing sales in non-
traditional outlets like health clubs and health food stores, and 3) the
largely untapped potential in the industrial and institutional markets.

"The continuing involvement of Americans in physical fitness has been a
plus in the energy drink market for a long time," said David A. Weiss,
Packaged Facts president. "Whether a person runs six miles a day or plays
three hard sets of tennis, he feels the need to replenish the mineral
salts and liquids in his body, and what more convenient way to do this
than to drink an energy drink especially formulated for this purpose.",

Fig. 3-2. News release. A good use of the logo, and of simple, typewriter produced graphics.

---

packaged facts
The Information Research Company

Consumer Market Studies

Food/Beverages

The Energy Drink Market

Will the rash of new competitors in the $250 million isotonic beverage market be able to successfully challenge the stranglehold that Quaker Oats' Gatorade has had on this market for so many years? Why have previous attempts failed? Can more be expected on the new marketers stirring up brand activity in this market – e Wagner Dragonade Recharge and Coca Cola's Max? This new Packaged Facts study brings the isotonic beverage market (and also the new hypertonic market) up to date starting with Stokely Van Camp's introduction of Gatorade in the 1960s, taking in the historical background to the present and analyzing the future market with its exceptional prospects for growth due to the ever expanding involvement of Americans in sports activity fitness, and health. Covered in The Energy Drink Market is successive order one detects tions of the products market size growth and projections the marketers (will and present the current competitive situation new product development advertising and promotion distribution and retail and consumer usage And as a special feature examples of advertising (both magazine and TV)
LA114 February 1987 85+ pages $995

The Diet Food Market

The new Packaged Facts study on the $1.4 billion diet food market is the most recent in a series that includes The Gourmet/Specialty Food Market and The Health & Natural Foods Market. Concentrating on foods related to weight loss, the study covers both low calorie and reduced calorie types. Overall growth factors including not only high-growth segments such as frozen diet foods but also low-growth segments such as canned fruits and vegetables, are analyzed. Special attention is paid to how market growth is maintained via a unique cyclic pattern which sees a particular product or product category skyrocket in sales, and then fade and another product zoom up in popularity to repeat the pattern.

Leading lines and brands are described, including Weight Watchers (Heinz); Stouffer's Lean Cuisine (Nestle); Classic Lite Frozen Dinners (ConAgra); NutraSweet (G. D. Searle); Nutrament (Bristol Myers); Slender (Carnation); Slim-Fast (Thompson Medical Group); Nutradiet (S & W); and Featherweight (Sandoz). Descriptions of the competitive situation market and product trends, advertising and promotion, distribution and retail and consumer usage are also included.
LA103 120 pages January 1987 145 pages $795

The Seafood Market

The comprehensive study from Packaged Facts summarizes in one report the three major segments of the $5.6 billion U.S. seafood market: fresh, frozen and canned. The study describes the overall market with special attention to the major factors affecting future sales—health and nutritional considerations, specific problems facing the $1.1 billion frozen and $2.0 billion canned fish markets and the trend toward "light"—and the leading marketers/brands—Mrs. Paul's, Gorton's, Van de Kamp, Star-Kist, Chicken of the Sea, Bumble Bee and Libby. The $2.7 billion fresh fish segment and the various factors affecting its sales, particularly supply and freshness, is also addressed by the analysis.

Each section covers products, market size and growth, factors in future growth, sales projections, market composition, the marketers, the competitive situation, company profiles, marketing and product trends, advertising and promotion, distribution and the situation at retail (margins, assortments, etc.) and consumer purchasing and shopping practices.
LA91 May 1986 250 pages $995

The Condiments Market

Steady growth characterizes this almost $3 billion market which includes ketchup mustard seafood sauces meat sauces barbecue sauces soy and other Oriental sauces chili sauce salt salt substitutes spices and seasonings (including extracts) pepper Mexican and hot sauces in this Packaged Facts market study both the overall market and the markets for each type of condiment are analyzed for growth—with special attention paid to the factors favoring and/or distavoring consumer sales

The competitive situation in each market segment is analyzed, the leading marketers are profiled (Heinz, R-T French, Hunt's, McCormick and Durkee). New products and new product trends are also discussed including the increasing popularity of gourmet mustards, recent shifts to more spicy and thicker sauces, stabilization of the spices market, introduction of salt alternatives as opposed to salt substitutes and new squeeze bottle packaging. Also covered is advertising and promotion, the situation at retail including pricing and consumer shopping patterns and attitudes. Included in the study are statistical tables charting market growth over the past five years and actual examples of advertising, both print and TV (in the form of storyboards)
LA87 September 1985 500 pages $995

Baby Food & Infant Formula Market

The Packaged Facts study examines the $2.4 billion market for baby food and infant formula. With a separate section on each type of product as well as an overview of the total market, the study zeroes in on the factors that will affect future growth—demographics, the extent of breast feeding spending patterns for new parents, dietary/nutritional concerns.

Sales figures as well as sales projections, are offered. Also covered are the competitive situation, packaging, advertising and promotion, the situation at retail and consumer usage and attitudes. Special attention is paid to product trends (in the case of baby food, products for the Hispanic market, acid reduced juice, instant baby food; health food for infants and salt and starch free infant food). The study contains numerous tables and charts, as well as profiles of leading marketers, including Gerber, Beech-Nut, Heinz, Ross Laboratories, Wyeth Laboratories, Mead Johnson and Coma Cinda Foods.
LA104 March 1987 100+ pages $1,150

The R-T-E Cereals Market

The Packaged Facts study is an updated version of the company's original 1984 study on the R-T-E cereals industry. It brings into focus the current state of the market by analyzing the significant changes that have taken place in this $4.5 billion market in the past three years—the mega-mergers affecting two of the industry's leaders (General Foods and Nabisco), the effect on the market of the continuing involvement of the American public in nutrition and fitness, recent demographic developments, breakfast trends in general, the economic appeal of cereals.

Pinpointed in the study are the various developments affecting both the market and the marketing of R-T-E cereals (the trend toward adult cereals and away from presweetened licensing). Sales projections and breakouts of sales by type are offered. Also covered is the competitive situation, new product trends, advertising, promotion, the situation at retail, consumer usage. The study contains numerous charts and tables and examples of advertising—magazine ads and TV storyboards.
LA105 February 1987 245 pages $1,150

Fig. 3-3. Order booklet. Eight pages, 8.5 × 11 inches, this is really a small catalog of reports. The final page has a coupon for ordering the reports.

Fig. 3-4. Even the notepads carry out the logo.

of a folder that would be about 4 inches by 9 inches when folded and trimmed. The outside could be an illustration, your logo, your picture or any combination of these on the front, with your return address and space for the prospect's address on the back.

Done on a word processor with a letter-quality proportional printer, it uses minimal artwork. However, if you can afford to have a picture taken of yourself, maybe working at your terminal, you could insert it, say, at the top right, deleting a paragraph or two. The printer will charge another five to ten dollars for shooting a half-tone of your picture. However, even with its heavy dependence on words, this brochure can be spruced up before printing. For instance, the printer's art department can draw boxes ("thin rules") around different sections of the brochure. All the bold type can be printed in black, while the other type is printed in another color or all type could be black, on colored paper.

When you have the look you want, you can concentrate on the words. Notice the text is specific, naming exactly the services offered. It focuses on the intended client's problems and questions and how your company responds to them. The sample is very generic, but you can use it to develop your own unique brochure.

Seminars and Conventions

The people in your target market will all belong to professional associations. America is association-rich. No market large enough to sustain your company will be without at least one association. This association will conduct a number of activities, including an annual meeting (or convention or seminar). You should be there.

The most popular approach to marketing at a convention is to rent a booth in the main hall and/or a hospitality suite upstairs and hand out expensive marketing material to everyone who comes within reach. Unfortunately, much of this expensive marketing material winds up in the hotel's "out basket." If you have too much money, feel free to try this approach. If, however, you don't have enough money, you can use other techniques.

*Fig. 3-5. Two more examples of logos
from information brokers.*

Every convention has featured speakers, though most conventions don't pay their speakers. Therefore, most speakers at conventions are rewarded in some other way. Often, they are rewarded by the exposure to a group of people who are their clients. You, too, would be rewarded by this kind of exposure to your potential clients. Moral? Be a featured speaker. You might even get them to waive the registration fee you'd probably have to pay otherwise.

You don't have to abandon the idea of an exhibit booth, either. Rent a smaller one and use it to gather information, not give it away. Purchase decisions are seldom made on the floor of a convention or in the hospitality suite. Purchase decisions are made back at the office. That's where you want your information in front of your potential client. What do you need to make this happen? A name and address. Here's how to get them.

Splurge for a case of good (but not great) wine and display it prominently in your booth. Schedule a drawing after the end of the convention to pick the name of the delegate who will win the case of wine. Hand out registration cards that also ask a few simple questions of the registrant, including name and address. Keep the completed registration cards for your mailing list, and remember to give away the case of wine.

If you want to sneak your advertising message home, number the registration cards and ask the registrants to keep their half of the card. On their half, print their number

What is Online Information Retrieval?

Online information retrieval is computer assisted access to over 300 databases covering business, the humanities, life sciences, technology, social sciences and current events. Many databases provide only references to magazines and newspaper articles; others cover conference papers, statistical data and technical reports. Many of the databases are also available as printed indexes in the Library and can often be efficiently searched manually.

What Do I Get?

Usually, the result of a search will yield references to articles (bibliographic citations). Some databases provide abstracts of articles and a few databases provide full text information, charts, and customized report formats for presentations. A printed copy of the search will be provided.

Why Should I Use It?

The computer can sift through thousands of references in seconds to retrieve the most relevant references. Through the computer, there is access to sources of information that are not available any other way.

What Does Online Information Retrieval Cost?

Online charges vary according to the database being searched. Database prices range from $35.00 to $300.00 per hour. An average search takes 15 minutes. Online search time, telecommunication costs and print charges are the responsibility of the patron. A $5.00 request fee and a surcharge of 10% of the total cost of the search is added to the online costs.

How Do I Use Online Information Retrieval?

Any Multnomah County Library card holder may come in person to the Catalog Information Desk, Second Floor, Central Library to request an online search.

- A request form for an in depth search will need to be completed

- A trained search analyst will arrange an interview. The arrangement for the interview may be made by phone if all the searchers are busy when you place the request.

- An interview is necessary to help the searcher refine terminology and plan a search strategy which will minimize the cost of the search.

- The searcher will explain the approximate costs of the search requested as nearly as can be determined at the end of the interview.

- The costs of a search must be paid by the patron at the conclusion of the search.

  (We regret that requests for online searching cannot be accepted by phone.)

For More Information About Online Information Retrieval Inquire at the

- Catalog Information Desk, Second Floor
  Central Library
  801 S.W. 10th Avenue
  Portland, OR 97205

Fig. 3-6. Multnomah County, Oregon library's booklet on information retrieval for patrons. Folded it is 6 × 9 inches, opened, it is 9 × 11 inches. White paper and two colors of ink (hot pink and deep purple) make it interesting.

INFORMATION SOLVES PROBLEMS!

Information can cause problems, when you don't have it. It can solve problems when it's there when you need it, in the right form. The right information gives you power.

You have to make tough business decisions: Should you expand now? Wait until the next fiscal year? Should you introduce that new product?

You have to control your business: Will your suppliers face problems in the future? What does the labor picture look like?

Pressures coming at you from all sides can tempt you to make decisions like this without complete information. But making decisions without information is asking for trouble, perhaps failure!

But information is only powerful in a form that is useful to you, delivered when you need it. That's why you need **KNOW NOW KNOW HOW,** the information research service.

WHAT DO YOU NEED TO KNOW?

Sometimes the problem is simply defining your problem. **KNOW NOW KNOW HOW** has the research experience to help you define exactly the data that will help you make the decisions that can make or break your business.

We use computerized data bases, full of statistics, news, trends and information. Some of it applies directly to you. A great deal of it will not. Using them can be expensive, if you are not familiar with their language.

We also have the expertise to do manual searching and original reasearch if you need it.

Getting the information that is important to you, quickly and efficiently, in a form that is pertinent and readable, is our job.

WHEN DO YOU NEED TO KNOW IT?

Once the data need is defined exactly, **KNOW NOW KNOW HOW** has the expertise to get it for you. Fast.

Too often, information reaches business people too late to help. Contracts have deadlines, stock markets close, time restrictions are everywhere. **KNOW NOW KNOW HOW** understands. We can give you raw data in less than a week. Edited data in 10 days. A completed report in two weeks. **While you do something else.**

HOW DO YOU NEED IT?

Our information services cover a wide range of forms.

◇ Instant Education gives you the background, history and current status on a subject. It can be in-depth, as in our 100-page reports on various topics. Or, it can be "quick and dirty" with only highlights.

◇ Current Awareness gives you regular updates on the news, changes and trends concerning a topic you need to know. Tailored to fit your market.

◇ Terse Topics can come up the with answer to your one-shot question: How many bananas were sold in the U. S. last year? What is the most popular color of car in France? **KNOW NOW KNOW HOW** can find out!

◇ Ready Reports can give you the latest statistical data available on the subject you choose.

WHERE DO YOU NEED IT?

We pride ourselves on delivery. We use every resource available to make sure you and your needed information get together.

WHO DO YOU NEED?

You need **KNOW HOW KNOW NOW,** of course. We're easy to find at 1234 Any Street in Your Town, ST. Or call us at (000)-555-1212. The information is out there. Let us bring it to you! Call or write us today!

**We can solve problems
FOR YOU!!**

Fig. 3-7. The beginning of a brochure. Less than and more than signs are used to form "diamonds"; bold type could be printed in a second color; the company's name is mentioned often.

and your advertising message. They won't throw away this handout and you'll make it back to their office. You then can take this new mailing list and send out a notice announcing the winner of the drawing and offering more information about your service. You'll be remembered and (in one case, at least) appreciated.

In addition to going to their seminars and workshops, you can also invite them to yours. Since business seminars are available through area libraries, through colleges and universities and commercially, you may want to consider offering your seminar/workshop through a local library or professional organization. Whether you charge and what you present is up to you, but you should wait until you have done some business and earned at least a little bit of credibility before trying this. Wait at least 3–6 months after beginning your business. A good topic is the benefits of online information in whatever subject area you search.

Keeping Clients

All of the discussion thus far has dealt with capturing new business. While getting new clients is important for any business, it is the only avenue open to a new business. But soon you will have clients and you will find that you want to keep them as clients. Satisfied customers simplify the process, and conventional wisdom says that it is cheaper and easier to retain a current client than to recruit a new one. What techniques can you use to keep your name in front of your satisfied customers?

In addition to the kinds of personal promotion noted above, you might offer to establish a "current awareness" service for someone with a continuing information need. Once you initially establish the question that this client needs answered and discover the appropriate sources for the answer(s) to that question, you can prepare a historical search of the databases and provide the client with a report. However, information continues to accumulate and databases are updated with new information, making the report the customer has received outdated. It is a fairly simple matter to re-search the appropriate databases as they are updated and provide the client with the information added since the last search. Some database vendors will automatically provide you this service. DIALOG calls it Selective Dissemination of Information (SDI) and it is available on many of their databases. If a service like SDI is not available from the vendor, you can run the search yourself using the same search parameters and terms from the original search, limiting it to new information.

If the nature of the client's search does not lend itself to a current awareness service, you might write to the client after some time has passed since the initial search and ask about the resolution of the situation that required your services. You can express your hope that all turned out well (and it will be a sincere hope, no doubt) and remind the client that you stand ready to be of service again. Some brokers electronically clip bits of information that might be of interest to a client and send it out as "For Your Information" material. This shows a client that you remember him and really do understand the nature of his business.

Another technique for encouraging repeat business (and for giving your cash flow a little more consistency) is the use of retainers. Under a retainer agreement, your client would deposit a sum of money with you and all charges would be paid out of this deposit. As the deposit amount declines, you would request additional money to replenish it. In return, your client would get, say, a lower hourly rate and/or priority service. You might also ask for a monthly fee charged to the retainer account. You would either charge this in addition to search fees or use it as a monthly minimum, charging it only if there was little account activity in a given month.

The cash flow advantages of this approach are explained very well by Chris Dobson of INFOMART:

> Set up your procedures for billing and collecting ahead of time. If possible, collect on delivery. Take credit cards. If you can get a retainer, take it—it encourages people to pay their bills and gives you a cushion when they don't. Invoicing is a real headache. Large, and some small, businesses routinely take 120 days to pay.

Ultimately, there is only one real key to retaining clients, and you already know what it is. If you don't promise more than you can deliver and if you deliver what you promised when you promised it at the price quoted, then you will get repeat business. If, however, you send out incomplete or inaccurate information in a sloppy format, late and overpriced, then you will not hear from that client a second time. You may hear from that client's attorney, but not from that client.

Having defined your market, product or service and pricing strategy, it's time to start looking at just how you decide how much to charge for your services.

Chapter 4

Fees and Charges

"**O**H, BOY, THIS'LL BE GREAT," YOU'RE THINKING. "IN MY CURRENT JOB, I'M MAKING $10 per hour and I've always heard that people working for themselves make a lot of money, so I'll charge $15 per hour and that'll be . . . let's see, 40 hours per week, 52 weeks per year . . . WOW!!! Practically $32,000 per year! That means if I charge $25 per hour, I could make over $50,000!" If that's what you're thinking, then this is the chapter for you.

This chapter will give you a process by which to figure your hourly rate, considering your work habits, your office and staffing arrangements and your salary goals. This is not a simple process. There is no magic hourly figure, and it is not enough just to charge about what your competition is charging. You will have operating costs, both fixed and variable, and you will have to pay these costs before you pay yourself. So, just picking what you'd like to make on an hourly basis is not the way to select your hourly rate.

Types of Expenses

First, a quick look at the two kinds of costs mentioned above: fixed and variable. The difference between the two is very simple. A fixed expense is an expense that is unchanged by the volume of business you do. A good example of a fixed expense is rent. If you rent an office, you will pay so much per month whether you have one client or a hundred. A variable expense is an expense which varies depending on the level of business you have. A good example of a variable expense is database costs. Your expense will certainly be greater if you have 100 active clients than if you have but one.

One nice thing about information brokering is that database access fees are one of the few major variable expenses you will have. Many brokers treat this expense as a pass-through expense (that is, an expense that is passed directly through to the client) and don't consider it as a part of their overhead when determining their hourly rate. This is an easy way to handle this expense (as opposed, say, to a flat hourly fee regardless of the databases searched), because it will place the greatest expense on those clients requiring the use of the most expensive databases.

Now this leaves a great many standard operating expenses unaccounted for: telephone, office supplies, printing, postage, insurance, professional services, salaries, transportation, promotion, membership dues, books and periodicals, and, of course, miscellaneous. You'll find you will have most, if not all, of these expenses, and you must account for them when setting your fees.

Setting Your Hourly Fee

In order to set your fees, you must know how much money you need; in order to know that, you must have a budget for your expenses. This budget, along with a few other guesses, will help you determine how much you should charge for your services.

Here is a sample (and very simple) monthly budget:

Rent	$250.00
Telephone	100.00
Printing & Postage	50.00
Marketing	500.00
Supplies	50.00
Miscellaneous	50.00
TOTAL	$1,000.00

This budget has nice, round numbers, unlike actual expenses, but it will serve to make the necessary points. You now have to figure how many of the hours you work will be billable hours and how many will be devoted to running the business.

For the sake of simplicity, assume that 50 percent of your time will be billable time and 50 percent will be non-billable time. The difference should be obvious. Billable time is time you spend actually working on a research project, time for which you can actually bill a client. Non-billable time is time you spend balancing your books, shuffling papers, and so on—time for which you cannot actually bill a client. If you figure 48 weeks per year (two weeks for vacation, after all, and two weeks for the various holidays, etc.) at five days per week, eight hours per day, then you can see that you will work 1,920 hours per year. If you will recall, 50 percent of these hours would be billable, giving you 960 hours to earn enough money to pay for your expenses and give you a profit.

Taking the $12,000 in expenses ($1,000 per month for 12 months) and dividing it by the 960 hours gives an hourly rate for expenses of $12.50. If you decide you would like to make $24,000 per year in profit, then you would divide that by the 960 hours to give an hourly rate for profit of $25. Now it is a simple matter to add these two hourly rates together to get a total hourly rate of $37.50. Plus database time, of course, since you decided that was a pass-through expense.

Does this mean that you should charge $37.50 per hour? No, of course not. The example chosen was very simple and assumed only a few basic expenses (no salary for other staff, no utilities, no benefits, etc.). The generalizations used here will not prove accurate in practice. You should spend some time planning how you will operate in order to make much better estimates than this one. The purpose here was to give you a basic idea of how to approach setting your fees, not to give you the magic number for your budget.

Start-Up Costs

Now that you have some idea of how to set your fees based on your operating costs, here's a look at how you can expect to spend some of your money getting started and staying started. Don't forget to account for these expenses when setting your hourly fee.

If you plan to work alone from an office in your home and can afford not to draw a salary for several months, then your start-up and initial operating costs can be kept fairly low. However, not many people are fortunate enough to be able to work for free for an extended period of time, and unless you are one who can, you will have to plan more carefully.

One of the most common financing errors made in new businesses is raising enough money to open the doors but not enough to operate the business until it begins to pay its own way. You will not be receiving income from day one. You may not even have a single client until your second or third month. Professionals generally advise that you have enough capital to open your doors and to operate for a minimum of six months. This will account for the time needed to get your initial clients, to do the work, to bill the client, to dun the client and, finally, to send a collection agency after the client. If in the meantime you have run out of cash, what are you going to do?

Make sure you don't go out of business simply because you didn't start with enough money. The expenses discussed so far are generally recurring expenses. That is, they are expenses you expect to have to pay every month. In starting a business, you will have to pay some expenses on a one-time basis, and you need to account for these expenses when you figure your cash flow, estimate the amount of start-up capital you will need, and set your fees.

In addition to paying your cost of operations and giving you a profit, your business should generate sufficient income to repay with interest the money initially invested to get you started. You should also have money to reinvest in the business, so that you can pay for unexpected items (your computer destroys itself), survive slow periods (all of your clients take vacation in August), and pay for business growth and expansion. All of this money has to come from your business earnings because you simply have no other ready source of funds.

Cash Flow

In your cash flow planning, don't expect to receive the money you earn in any given month in that same month. Most businesses operate on a monthly billing arrangement, so plan to earn it one month, bill it at the end of that month and receive it, maybe, by the end of the next month. You may want to consider working on a partial or full "payment up front" basis, and using credit cards or certified checks for all but your best clients. These decisions are left to your discretion, but unless you operate strictly C.O.D., plan for some lag between the date money is earned and the date it is received.

Certain techniques can speed the collection process. The primary technique is to be candid about your expectations of payment. If you have your client sign an agreement of any kind, include your collection policy in that agreement (payment due by 10th of month following billing) and then be consistent in your billing and collection practices.

You might collect a deposit against the full cost of the search before you begin work or, if the client resists that, deliver the work C.O.D. Be careful when using these methods that you do not suggest that the client is in any way untrustworthy; explain that this is your standard policy. Of course, if your client *is* untrustworthy, reconsider your decision to accept the assignment.

Retainers, as discussed earlier, also help give consistency to your cash flow. The retainer will work only with your regular customers (though it is a good way to make new customers into regular customers). For one-time-only sales, you might want to be able to accept credit cards. You'll need to bank where you can get merchant status (required for you to be able to accept Visa or MasterCard), so shop around for a bank that will work with you on this. Also, shop around for the best rates. You will be charged a percentage, set by the bank, of each credit card sale. If you do a lot of credit card business, you'll save a significant amount of money by finding the best rate.

Equipment and Book Costs

You may already own much of the computer hardware and software you are going to need to be an information broker. If not, then it should be pretty obvious that you are going to have to buy, rent, or lease a dumb communicating terminal (at the very least). A tremendous variety of hardware and software at a wide range of prices is available to you. Suffice it to say that you must let the uses to which you will put the equipment and software determine your selection. To do otherwise is folly.

If you don't own a computer and are unsure of how to go about buying one, here's a short course in computer purchasing, introduced in Chapter 2. First, decide in some detail what you want the computer to do. Be thorough and plan, not just for the present, but for the future. Once you have decided what you want the computer to do, find out which software will do what you need. Compare programs with similar claims and find out which ones work for you. Then, once you have chosen your software, buy a computer that will run that software. Don't buy the hardware first and then try to find useful software for it. That is backwards.

Many of your operating expenses are going to be those common in any small business, and they won't be discussed in detail here. If you have consulted the Small Business Administration or taken a business course, you know what these expenses are. If you have not contacted the SBA or taken a business course, do so. Certain other expenses are peculiar to information brokering, and they will be discussed here.

When you first thought about becoming an information broker, you were probably at least a little excited by the prospect of having a paperless office. Don't be too disappointed, but one of your greatest expenses will be for paper: instructional and operational manuals and reference books. You see, as wonderful as all of these computer databases are, they are essentially useless unless you know how and where to ask for what you need to know.

You will use books and manuals, not only to do some research, but also to determine how best to do the research. Unless you are intimately familiar with a database, you won't want to sign on and browse for the information you need. You should do a bit of study on how the database is structured, what "hooks" it offers you for finding the necessary information and how it stores the information you need. Your only other option is to waste time floundering around, hoping to chance upon the information you require. One of the things you have to sell is efficiency, so you must be efficient.

Another major expense of this type is training. Most of the larger database vendors offer some form of training for their systems. DIALOG Information Systems, for instance, offers a full range of courses from their day long introductory course ($125 in late 1987) to day-long and half-day advanced subject seminars in areas such as Science & Technology (day-long, $125) and Company Intelligence (half-day, $55). Even if you only sign up for a few sessions, you can see how quickly this can add up. Take the training anyway. You'll save more than you spend.

There's another cost associated with having access to databases. Some database vendors will charge you a minimum monthly fee regardless of whether you use the system. If you do use the system, then this fee often is applied to your usage, but you pay it in any case. Other services not only charge you a monthly minimum but a monthly "privilege of being a subscriber" fee. You pay this fee every month whether you use the service or not. You may be able to avoid signing on with one of these vendors (at first, at least), but you may want to be able to offer that service to your clients as an added value.

The True Cost of Information

The competition among the various database vendors has yet to lead to anything significant in pricing competition. Prices for the various databases and services are set according to different rules and it may be hard for you to understand why a given database costs as much as it does. Particularly in a service economy, perceived value often has more to do with price than does cost of production.

It is hard to pin a specific value on information. The United States traditionally thinks of information as free and believes that it should be universally available. You might agree that information should be free. In reality, information is never free. You may have to explain to your client, for example, that information available from the local public library is not free. First, there is the cost of building, stocking, operating, and maintaining the library itself—a very expensive proposition paid for by tax dollars. Then there is the cost of having somebody go to the library and find and retrieve the information. This, too, costs money. And there is the cost of collecting and publishing that information so that it can be in the library to start with.

Online time, however, appears to be much more expensive than the time spent in the public library, and in almost every case, on an hourly basis, it is. Maybe, in time, one or more of the major online vendors will try a different pricing strategy, lowering its unit cost in hopes of attracting a much larger client base. Hidden costs, however, work against that decision. For instance, no service could accommodate even a doubling of its current usage without having to add equipment. The kinds of computers used by the database vendors are very expensive; low-cost clones of mainframes do not exist. Part of what keeps prices high might be the fear of what would happen if everybody really did start using the service. A major capital expansion would be required and, in the interim, the system response time would be totally unacceptable. It may seem odd that a fear of too much success helps keep prices high, but many companies have failed because they did not manage their growth.

One way of determining the value of information is to look at the cost of not having that information. For an attorney, for instance, the cost of not knowing about an important precedent might be very high while the cost of an online search to find it would be comparatively low. You may find some clients have trouble understanding the relationship between the cost of information and the value of that information. You'll recall that much of the information you'll be searching will be information developed by other people. These other people developed this information because they saw value in that information. The value lies in the usefulness of that information to the party who paid for its initial development and to the parties who pay to find it.

As a consequence of this, something of an inverse relationship exists between the value of secondary information and its acquisition cost. Information that is of low value will probably have a relatively high cost, simply because nobody has bothered to develop that information before. Information that is of high value may have a relatively low cost because more people are willing to pay more money to develop it and then make it available, online or in print.

While you don't want to spend too much of your valuable marketing time educating potential clients about the importance of information, it would be a mistake to assume their understanding of the costs and value of information is as thorough as yours. Be sensitive to their perspectives, but don't embark on a new career as a volunteer educator.

Estimating Search Costs

Once you've established your basic fee structure and you're out aggressively marketing your service, you may encounter an unexpected problem. Your first client calls and you go to her office to discuss the project. She outlines the situation, you show her how you can give her the information she needs and then she asks, "How much is this going to cost?" At this point, she's not interested in your hourly rate, the online costs of the various database services and the report preparation fee. She wants just one figure—how much is this going to cost?

How do you come up with a number for her? You'll need a number that will allow you the latitude you need to conduct a thorough search and still make a profit, and a number that will be acceptable to her. Estimating search costs is not easy, but it usually has to be done. Information brokers handle this situation in a number of ways.

One way to postpone having to deal with this situation is to offer to provide an estimate within a set period of time following this initial interview. ("I'll get back to you.") While this allows you time to develop a more accurate estimate, it also prevents you from making the sale on the spot. You can offer a range of costs in order to get general approval for the work and then supply a more specific estimate a bit later. You also can turn the tables and ask the client what she was ready to spend on the job. You can justify this by explaining that you can do the job at various expense levels, depending on the detail and thoroughness required by the client.

Sooner or later, however, you're going to have to come up with a number. You know by now the various elements that will contribute to this number, and you should make your estimates by considering each element and how much it will cost. As you gain experience, you may learn to give fairly accurate general estimates quickly, but, at first, you should take your time in figuring your cost estimates.

You can always set a cost beyond which you will not go without permission. It should be high enough to allow you some solid results in case your client decides to stop there. If you reach the limit, you can tell your client what you have so far, estimate what else might be out there, and set another, higher, plateau price. This process can be repeated, but not so many times that you abuse your client's patience. Bob Sherman, of C.A.R.O.L., relates the following tale of cost estimating:

> We try to give a "ballpark estimate" when asked. We explain our price policy and what we think it should run. We then give them an option of setting a cutoff point where we will not go beyond without reporting back to the client. In other words, if we estimate $200, the client may say, "OK, but do not go above $250." So we stop at that point and call them with a progress report, and how much more we think the project will cost to complete. They either say, "Go ahead," or "Stop there and send us what you have to this point only." An example was a recent request for every story in print in the London Financial Times on a certain company. We found 354 stories back to 1980, realized that offline prints would run between $300–$500 alone, not including what we had already done on the project. We stopped right there, and called the client, told them what the charges were so far, and how much that one little part of the entire project would

cost. They gave the go ahead, and on top of that, wanted the entire printout Fed Ex'd overnight to them for another $50 or so. The total job ran about $750, and they were quite happy (the client was a law office readying legal action against the company in question).

Melissa Kirkpatrick of Cassandra Associates, an editorial and research service in Reston, VA, has developed the following explanation of the costs associated with online searching:

Researcher's Time—Usually per hour, this includes developing research strategy with client. Also offline preparation. Will not parallel connect time.

Telecommunications Charges—Generally billed with online connect charges at rate of $12–$15 per hour.

Online Connect Charges—Differ from one database to another.

Data Display Charges—Vary by database and format of data displayed. Charges usually encompassed in online connect charges.

Document Delivery Charges—Most immediate is online printing. Some can be printed offline and mailed. Specialty reports may have extra surcharges. Some documents can be obtained through document delivery service (charges vary, but average $14–$18 per document). Time permitting, your staff can retrieve available documents identified in online bibliographic search.

Final Words of Advice

Finally, a few words of advice about spending your money and setting your fees.

Is it all right to charge a lower fee initially so as to build up business? To answer that question with a question, do you really want to build up a large clientele that has come to expect a fee lower than it ought to be? Set your fees where they belong. If absolutely necessary, you can offer someone an introductory discount off the normal rate, but choosing to set your fee too low is not good judgement.

Isn't it cheaper to do everything myself, at least at first? That all depends on your talents. If you are an attorney, CPA, graphic artist, layout artist, manager, salesperson, researcher, clerk/typist and courier, then maybe you can do it all yourself. If, however, you are like most people and have some strengths and some weaknesses, then you may be better off hiring some temporary or part-time help (or using a service) to do those things that you should not do yourself. And it cannot be said too many times— get a lawyer and get an accountant. Do it now.

If you are a wretched typist, why spend all day (and night) typing some report or proposal when you could hire another person to do the typing while you spend the day getting a new client or doing billable research (and spend the night sleeping)? Use your good judgement and remember that while it is initially harder to delegate than it is to do it yourself, it will pay off in the long run in a more successful business and a more well-adjusted you.

Chapter 5

Legal Considerations

GOING INTO BUSINESS TODAY IS, AMONG MANY OTHER THINGS, A COMPLEX LEGAL process. In addition to the obvious examples, such as incorporation, many steps require you to think of the legal requirements and ramifications of your decisions. Information brokering shares many of the steps that are common to all businesses, and it has a few unique ones. Without any doubt, you should consult with your attorney about these steps. He will be familiar with those that are universal and this chapter will deal only with those peculiar to information brokering.

This chapter (indeed this entire book) should not be considered legal advice. In all questions of this type you should seek the counsel of an attorney. What is offered here is simply an overview of some of the areas of concern within the information brokering business and an examination of how some participants deal with them. Again, this is not legal advice and should not be relied on as such. See your lawyer.

Copyright

As soon as people consider the information business, they wonder about the question of copyright. Yet the experts say this is not a significant problem. An old saw among authors goes, "If you use one source, it's plagiarism. If you use three, it's research." This is a new way to do research, but it doesn't change the rules.

Two important concepts here are the form of information and the awareness of what, exactly, you are selling.

As to the latter, as an information broker you sell your expertise, time, and ability to use information resources. An overworked hypothetical question asks, "What happens if two clients ask identical questions?" It takes as much expertise to answer that question for Client A as for Client B; that expertise is your product. But don't forget that the database is the vendor's and producer's product. Some vendors or producers may not be willing to be wholesalers. In practice you will probably never encounter two clients with identical information needs. Each client has specific needs, and only if his direct competition called might you be required to perform the same search twice. But in theory it is something to be considered carefully. Don't sell the results of the same search twice. One search, one sale may be the safest way to play it. It may clarify things at this point to quote from a letter dated April 20, 1984 written by DIALOG's attorney, Robert A. Simons.

> We view information brokering not as re-selling of search output but, as an activity whereby the search intermediary acts on behalf of an ultimate client insofar as research is concerned. Thus, in the typical case, the search output goes to the ultimate client, who reimburses the information broker for the out-of-pocket expenses of the search and pays the customary service fees as established by the information broker.
>
> So long as each search for each client is performed on a case-by-case basis with no systematic photocopying and redistribution of the search output, we are not aware that any copyright law has been violated. As a policy, we will grant information brokers permission to use DIALOG Service search output in this fashion, subject to acquiring like permission from our database suppliers and subject further to strict compliance with copyright law. We also insist that the ultimate client be informed of and, as between the ultimate client and information broker, agree to the terms and conditions then applicable to the use of the DIALOG Service. . . .
>
> . . . It has been our experience that information brokers are routinely granted permission from database suppliers, so long as assurances against photocopying/copyright law infringement are provided. . . . At the present time, we are not granting like permission with respect to usage of our KNOWLEDGE INDEX Service, which . . . is intended for true end users. . . .
>
> . . . It is imperative that a person who is interested in becoming an information broker seek expert legal counsel in the area of copyright law.

This position was reaffirmed by Mr. Simons in a letter dated August 26, 1987. In this letter, Mr. Simons also calls attention to the specific restriction on World Patents Index from Derwent Publications, Ltd. In the "Database Supplier Terms and Conditions" provided by DIALOG, Derwent includes the following:

- That, in the event the customer wished to conduct searches on behalf of third parties, then the customer will notify Derwent to this effect confirming that all the conditions of these provisions will be adhered to. Searching for third parties will not be permitted until permission has been confirmed by Derwent in writing.

- Any search carried out for a third party will be performed directly by the customer's employees only and will be solely for that third party.

- Any search conducted for a third party will be solely for that third party, who will undertake that the results of such a search are for their own internal use only.

- Whenever the customer obtains information from the Derwent database for a third party, customer shall make acknowledgment to the third party of the ownership by Derwent of the data concerned and all rights therein.

The form of information is copyrightable, but not the information itself, according to publisher Norm Goode. In his series on information brokering published in ''Micro Moonlighter Newsletter,'' Goode writes,

> When a literary work is copyrighted only the actual words themselves are protected. Facts cannot be copyrighted. . . If I have a need for a bibliography in order to be able to research a specific writing project, I may choose to access the Books-In-Print section of DIALOG or BRS. The facts found (the list of books on a particular subject) are not copyrightable.
>
> The format of the listings, including the prompts for each information field about a book, is the property of R.R. Bowker (the originator of Books-In-Print). I may use the list of books in any way I wish as long as I do not duplicate the format of the Books-In-Print database. . .
>
> Most communications packages have the ability to store captured data in ASCII (plain text) format. This same format should also be compatible with your word processing software. By loading the data captured from the online service into your word processor, you then have the capability to alter, rearrange, (add to from other sources) and modify the format of the facts to conform to your own special use or that of your client. Hence, you have made use of only the facts garnered—not the copyrightable material. So, to answer everyone's question. . . you cannot resell the information as captured from the database; but you can resell the facts, statistics, etc., gained from any search.

In some cases, you may feel the form is perfect, and that your client deserves to see it as you found it. In that case, according to Kelly Warnken in *The Information Brokers*, you may need to pay the originator a copyright fee, and pass that cost on to the client.

Bob Sherman of C.A.R.O.L. notes that ''several database vendors have required us to sign special contracts and pay higher rates to cover their copyrights.'' The usual vendor contracts require that their information not be resold, but if you identify yourself, your business and your purpose, this can be waived.

Different databases respond differently to this issue. Most seem concerned that you do not download a significant portion (or all) of a database and offer it for resale. Since, in practice, the amount of information they have is so vast, and the needs an information broker brings to it so specific, you may not see why you should have the inclination. But as mass storage becomes more available to micros, particularly on the Write Once, Read Many times (or WORM) optical disks, it will become easier to download an entire file, or a substantial portion of one, and then search it at your leisure offline.

INSPEC, from the Institution of Electrical Engineers, has a document, "Downloading from the INSPEC Database," which says, in part:

> An information broker who carries out a search of the INSPEC Database on behalf of a client may supply a printed copy of the results to that client.

No additional charge, over and above the normal online and royalty charges is made for this . . . use. Such use is now included in the statement of allowed uses which INSPEC requires online hosts to include in customer contracts.

In the appendix you will find letters from database vendors and producers, stating their policies on this issue.

Different rules of copyright apply in the area of document delivery. If you're going to be in the business of photocopying source documents and delivering those photocopies to your clients, you have a different copyright obligation. By law, you are required to pay a royalty fee for the copying of the documents. Fortunately, you don't have to chase all over the country to seek out publishers so you can pay them tiny sums of money. An organization exists to do that for you—the Copyright Clearance Center (CCC).

For those publishers who are members of the CCC (and most major publishers are), you simply send in a monthly statement of the articles you've copied and the publishers of those articles along with a fee for those copies. The CCC takes care of sending each publisher a fair share of that money. There are other site-license programs available from the CCC, but these are expensive and would be inappropriate for any but the largest document delivery services. Check with the CCC for details to avoid potential problems down the line. Unfortunately, for those publishers who are not members of CCC, you'll have to negotiate individual agreements.

Contractual Liability

Another common concern is liability. Most experts agree that you are not liable for the accuracy of the information you discover and supply to your client, nor for the consequences your client may suffer because of the information. If you have honestly and fairly delivered the service, your contractual liability has been satisfied. While that fact might help you prevail in court, being in the right is no guarantee you won't be sued.

Ed Marsh, Ph.D., director of the Small Business Development Center at Alabama A&M in Huntsville, Ala., put it this way,

> You are contracting to perform a service, one reason the copyright is not a problem. Oral contracts are just as binding as written ones, but harder to prove, of course. A written agreement or statement of work protects both sides. It should specify the sources of the search, means and cost. The basis is mutuality of obligation; you to perform, the client to pay.

You are performing research for someone on a topic for a fee. The astute client will require a dollar limit, Marsh said, and especially in the beginning you might want to absorb cost overruns (put it under the heading, "I'll know better next time."). As an alternative, if you see you are running close to the limit, contact your client, state what has been done and what more needs to be done. Marsh noted that most cases deciding on fraud use the absence of such notification as a sign of intent to deceive. Putting this in a written contract will also help your legal position later should you have trouble collecting.

However, the psychology of the situation should be carefully considered. A contract, especially one full of Latin and legalese, may only serve to alarm the client. The small business or individual client, or one whose search is a one-shot and simple affair, may see it as a lack of trust on your part; some may see it as a sign you have ulterior motives.

A *letter of agreement* will probably be something to consider in many cases. A letter of agreement is simply a letter, on your letterhead or the client's, that states the agreement: exactly what service and product is to be produced and in what time period, the amount and basis of the charges (whether flat or hourly), and the invoicing method (full payment in advance, monthly billing in triplicate, or whatever).

Figures 5–1, 5–2 and 5–3, respectively, offer a sample contract, a sample letter of agreement and sample *supplemental terms and conditions*. These are good starting points should you wish to use such forms of agreement. Adapt them to your situation.

In thinking about how you want to approach the question of liability for the results of your research, you should take a look at what other information companies are doing to limit their liability. For instance, Easynet, from Telebase Systems, displays the following disclaimer when you run a search on their system:

> We have no reason to believe that errors exist in the data or services furnished. If there are any such errors the parties hereto have no liability for any consequential, incidental or punitive damages. No warranty, either expressed or implied, including but not limited to those of merchantability or fitness for a particular purpose are made. Any liability is limited to the amount paid by the customer to EasyNet . . .

The DIALOG Bluesheets (summary sheets on each of DIALOG's databases) are another good source for the language of limited liability. Consider the following, taken from a few bluesheets chosen at random:

> BioSciences Information Service makes a diligent effort to provide complete and accurate representation of the bioscientific literature in its information services but assumes no liability for errors and omissions . . .

> Standard & Poor's obtains information for inclusion in the database from sources which it considers reliable, but Standard & Poor's does not guarantee the accuracy or completeness of the Database or of any information contained therein. Standard & Poor's makes no warranties, express or implied, as to results to be obtained by any person or entity from the use of the Database and makes no warranties of merchantability or fitness for a particular purpose. Standard & Poor's shall have no liability for lost profits or indirect or consequential damages . . .

> While every attempt has been made to ensure the accuracy of the database, Disclosure Information Group makes no warranties or representations regarding its accuracy, completeness, merchantability, or fitness for use and each subscriber to or user of the

BETWEEN _____ (THE BUYER)

AND: _____ (THE SELLER)

1. Seller is to provide research as applicable to the Buyer's information requirement. These services are to be provided, generally, on site at the Seller's facilities, at the following rates:

    Service category   Rate

2. Performance shall begin on or about _____ and shall extend through _____; Buyer has the option to extend the period of performance as determined by mutual negotiations between the Buyer and the Seller.

3. The Supplemental Terms and Conditions on the reverse side of this document are made a part of this Agreement; and in the event of conflict between items 1 through 3 above and the Supplemental Terms and Conditions, Items 1 through 3 above shall govern.

4. Buyer's acceptance must be limited to these terms and the Supplemental Terms and Conditions. A purchase order, confirmation, or other similar response from Buyer which contains any additional, different or inconsistent terms will be considered only as an acceptance of the terms set forth herein; and such additional, different or inconsistent terms shall not be binding on Seller without Seller's express written consent.

Fig. 5-1. Sample contract.

product understands that Disclosure Information Group disclaims any liability for any damages (even if Disclosure Information Group has been advised of such damages) in connection with its use . . .

Neither SEP, nor its contractors nor any person or agency acting on its behalf accept any responsibility for the accuracy of the data contained in the database, or for the way the same have been collected, filed and/or processed . . .

The database supplier represents that the database provided hereunder was formulated with a reasonable standard of care and in conformance to professional standards in the field. Except with respect to the foregoing and as otherwise specifically provided in this agreement, the database supplier makes no representations or warranties, express or implied, including, but not limited to any implied warranty of merchantability or fitness for a particular purpose, with respect to such databases and specifically disclaims all such warranties and representations.

John Jones
ABC Company
54321 Any Street
Newtown ST 00000

Dear Mr. Jones,

After our conversation on Monday the 14th, I would like to summarize the project as follows:

Project: A bibliography of articles and books that address the subject of Information Brokering.

Deadline: Monday, May 28, 1984, close of business.

Payment: $300 payable in advance, plus expenses as presented by invoice.

Thank you for your business.

Sincerely,

Wanda Hacker
Know Now Know How

Fig. 5-2. Sample letter of agreement.

In addition to the disclaimers of the database producers, it is also interesting to review those of the database vendors, as well. The subscription order form for BRS Information Technologies contains the following terms and conditions:

> • The BRS/SEARCH Service is made available on an "AS IS BASIS." BRS AND ITS DATABASE SUPPLIERS MAKE NO WARRANTIES OR REPRESENTATIONS OF ANY KIND, EXPRESS OR IMPLIED, INCLUDING BUT NOT LIMITED TO WARRANTIES OF MERCHANTABILITY OR FITNESS FOR A PARTICULAR PURPOSE. NEITHER BRS NOR ITS DATABASE SUPPLIERS SHALL BE RESPONSIBLE FOR INCIDENTAL, CONSEQUENTIAL OR ANY OTHER DAMAGES ARISING OUT OF OR IN CONNECTION WITH THE SERVICE OR MATERIALS PROVIDED HEREUNDER OR THIS AGREEMENT. [Emphasis in original].

> • The Customer assumes the sole responsibility for all use of the BRS/SEARCH Service and agrees to indemnify and hold BRS and its database suppliers harmless from any liability or claim of any person arising for the Customer's use of the services or materials provided hereunder.

The exact nature and limitations of liability in this area will one day be more clearly defined by the courts. Stating that you are not liable for damages does not guarantee

1. Any use of the report provided by (company name) other than for the internal uses provided for in this contract is prohibited. Resale or other commercial use of this report is also prohibited. Any violation of this condition may be a copyright or proprietary right infringement and can result in legal action being taken against you.

2. The use of and reliance on any information provided by (company name) is at your own risk and discretion. (Company name) makes no assurances as to the merchantability or fitness for a specific purpose of this information. (Company name) shall not be responsible for any damages resulting from mistakes, omissions, errors, delays or other defects in the information provided, or for any performance defect due to circumstances beyond the control of (company name). You hereby indemnify (company name) against any claim for damages or loss (including any and all legal costs) resulting from your misuse of this information (including copyrights and proprietary rights). This indemnification shall not terminate with the termination of this service contract.

3. (Company Name) will make every effort to locate the requested information and to check the accuracy of the information provided to the client, and will indicate all sources consulted. However, (Company Name) makes no warranty as to the accuracy or completeness of the printed information provided to the client.

4. (Company Name) shall take all reasonable steps to insure that all requests for information by the client are kept confidential.

5. (Company Name)'s charges are based on an hourly fee plus out of pocket expenses, which can include long distance phone charges, computer costs, postage, and direct purchase of materials. A two hour minimum labor charge applies to each research project.

6. (Company Name) will, in respect of any particular request for information, either provide a quotation before processing request, or accept a limit upon which the charges to be incurred which limit can only be exceeded with the client's authorization. The client accepts that such a limit may mean that the information provided by (Company Name) in response to the request will be only such information as (Company Name) is able to research within the time constraints such a limit imposes.

7. (Company Name)'s charges are payable within 30 days of invoice (Company name) has the right to impose a 1.5% per month overdue charge on any balances past due by 30 days or more.

8. (Company Name) makes every effort to compile information in accordance with its customers' requests and specifications. However, since it does not prepare the underlying records and documents, copies of which are enclosed herewith, it does not guarantee the accuracy or completeness of the information contained therein. It is, therefore, not liable for any errors or omissions in the enclosed compilation.

9. Any addition to, amendment of or cancellation of this agreement must be in writing and signed by the parties to this agreement. No agreements, warranties, or other understandings exist between the two parties to this agreement other than those contained in writing in this agreement.

Fig. 5-3. Sample supplemental terms and conditions.

that you are not liable for damages. You may be familiar with a case or two in this area of law. A company might sue the publisher of a spreadsheet program because a bug in that program caused incorrect output and, relying on that output, the company underbid a contract, resulting in a loss of money. In that same vein, your client, relying on the results of a search you performed, might make a faulty decision (due to a deficiency in the database, not to any fault of yours) and choose to sue you for damages.

What is clear from the wide variance in the use of disclaimers and in the content of those disclaimers is that this area of law is not yet precisely defined. It may never be, but it will be well worth your while to seek and follow competent legal advice on this point.

Conclusions

There are never simple, clear answers to business legal questions. This book cannot prepare you for every legal eventuality you may face, nor can it give you a "fill-in-the-blanks" approach to operating your business. Such a goal would be beyond the scope of any book because your needs will be unique to your situation. Going it alone generally is not the best approach, either.

Professional legal help, despite its high cost, can help you avoid pitfalls such as trouble with the IRS, disagreement over dissolution of a partnership, and regret for something you had or had not done. This is a good investment in your future: the legal woods are not a good place in which to be a babe. The consequences of being unprepared in this area can be grave, and this chapter is only a summary. For specifics, get professional advice.

Chapter 6

Technological Considerations

NOBODY DOUBTS THAT TECHNOLOGY PLAYS AN IMPORTANT ROLE IN INFORMATION BRO-kering. And as technology changes, the rules change as well. You should be aware of some of the technological changes in the information industry and you also should be aware that change will continue as new technologies emerge and old ones are improved.

However, one very important point must be made right now: technology is not your business—information is your business. The information industry, in fact, is often technology-driven instead of market-driven. This is backwards. To be as successful as you can be, you must make decisions based on your market, not on technological or other peripheral considerations. You are selling information and expertise, not CD-ROMs, baud rates, storage capacity or laser printing. Information and expertise must be at the forefront of your thinking and working. If you are preoccupied with technology, you could make serious mistakes in judgment. This gets back to the question of what business you are in, and you just are not in the technology business.

Now, with that caveat, it's time to explore the newest tools of the trade. The information industry is intensely interested in three areas in late 1987. They are CD-ROM technology, front-end search software and services, and the increase in full-text databases.

CD-ROM

CD-ROM (for Compact Disk Read-Only Memory) technology offers a world of information on a 12-centimeter silver platter, the same kind of silver platter that brings audiophiles the world of Beethoven or Madonna. On one side of a compact disk you can store 540 megabytes of information, the equivalent of 1,500 floppy disks or about 250,000 typewritten pages (all depending on a number of assumptions about how the information is stored on the disk). This storage capacity represents tremendous opportunities for the transmission, storage and retrieval of information.

Databases now available on compact disk include Books-in-Print, Disclosure, ERIC, Medline, Ulrich's Plus, LC Marc, Grolier's Electronic Encyclopedia, and Agricola. Companies with compact disks on the market include DIALOG, H.W. Wilson, Microsoft, Bowker, Disclosure, Duns, Datext, and SilverPlatter. This list is not complete and, even if it were at the time of writing, it would be incomplete by the date of publication. The field is growing rapidly and continuously.

And, while there are many CD-ROM products on the market, there are even more opinions on how CD-ROMs should be used in the information industry. This is a topic of great interest to everyone who buys, sells, finds, uses or processes information, including information brokers. What is of greatest interest is not the specifics of the technology, but the market implications for the broker in a world where CD-ROMs are common. This section will offer you a little help in developing your thoughts on this subject.

When CD-ROM began its career as a buzz word, it seemed a solution in search of a problem. The information industry is heavily influenced (maybe controlled?) by technology and this new technology had a lot of people excited. No one was quite sure what it would be used for, but they were all sure it would revolutionize the information industry.

The early projections were, as it turned out, a bit overstated. While there has been a lot of progress in CD-ROM technology and, more importantly, the useful application of that technology, there has been no upheaval in the field of information as a result. The changes are more evolutionary than revolutionary.

So, what does CD-ROM mean to you? A lot of people have looked foolish trying to predict the future of CD-ROM, but you can reach a few conclusions, based on the current state of development of the technology.

First, what won't happen. All of your clients (or potential clients) are not going to run out and buy CD-ROM drives and a library of disks, thus making you and your service obsolete. If the people who use information were so interested in personally gathering the information they need, they would all have DIALOG passwords today. Second, CD-ROM publishing will not replace online databases. Files that are frequently updated are not suited for CD-ROM distribution and, for all their marvelous storage capacity, CD-ROMs are not appropriate for large, full-text databases. And, third, while CD-ROMs offer a viable distribution method for narrow, vertical information products, the broad, general-interest databases still can be effectively distributed online.

The harder question is, "What will happen?" By taking a look at some of the characteristics of CD-ROMs, it is possible to make some projections about their eventual role in the marketplace and, in turn, to estimate the effect of this new technology on information brokering.

There are several areas of information transmission, storage, and retrieval that would benefit from the use of CD-ROMs. Vertical market databases, where the number of users is not large enough to attract the interest of database services such as BRS and DIALOG, could use CD-ROM to efficiently distribute their information. Any market that could attract at least 100 users could justify the expense of creating a CD-ROM product —presuming, of course, that the information is valuable enough to justify a premium price.

A key to this use of CD-ROM technology is the availability of quality search and retrieval software for use with the information on the CD-ROM. If each publisher must individually create proprietary search software designed to work with that specific information product, the development costs will be too high for many would-be publishers. Once standard search software is available and in wide use, this barrier will be eliminated. One kind of search software being developed for use with CD-ROMs is known generally as hypertext. Hypertext attempts to link information in a manner that is similar to the way people think about information. If hypertext becomes an affordable reality, any number of CD-ROM information products will be able to take advantage of it.

A second area where CD-ROMs have a definite role is in the distribution of the more static databases. Grolier's Electronic Encyclopedia is an excellent example of this. The cost of reprinting and redistributing an encyclopedia is tremendous, making the cost of reproducing and redistributing a CD-ROM version of that same encyclopedia much more attractive. Another example is REMARC, the retrospective file of the works cataloged by the Library of Congress from 1897 to 1978. Once REMARC is complete, there will be no need for updating. A static information product is perfectly suited for distribution on CD-ROM.

Even with information products that are not static, there will be attempts to combine CD-ROM versions of the database with online updating. In this way, a client could search, at leisure, a CD-ROM database of, say, financial information. Then once the information available on the CD-ROM had been located and extracted, an online search (with the search strategy clearly defined during the CD-ROM search) could be run to capture the most current data available on the subject. This approach offers the advantage of limited online costs. Not only is the CD-ROM available as a flat-fee product, but it also eliminates much of the online cost, both by providing much of the information and by allowing refinement of the search strategy before the online meter kicks in.

One way, then, in which you could benefit from CD-ROM technology, is by using CD-ROM databases in the same way as the end user would. If you use or plan to use one database frequently enough, it would pay for you to purchase the CD-ROM version of that database, either as a stand-alone product or as part of a CD-ROM/online package. This might even give you a marketing edge by allowing you to offer a flat-rate search charge to your clients. And, as Chris Dobson notes, "Flat fees are much more attractive to customers than 'that depends.' " While there is still a great deal of discussion about who owns the information published on CD-ROM, Susan Willner of Disclosure, Inc., says, "Our policies for downloading information from Compact Disclosure parallel those for the various online systems. In other words, if the downloading and resupplying of the data is a one-time occurrence, then Disclosure would generally grant the user (broker) permission." Since you can search your CD-ROM as often as you like without incurring any additional cost, that statement would seem to encourage this kind of use of a CD-ROM database (at least Compact Disclosure).

One word of caution, however: a database available on more than one online service may not be the same database on each service. The breadth or depth of coverage might be different; frequency and currency of updates might vary. The same holds true with CD-ROMs. A compact disk version of a database may not be the same as an online version of that same database. In fact, coverage is often a bit more selective. For instance, the Investext files available on Datext's CD/Corporate are no more than 3 years old while the online database (on DIALOG) includes records back to 1982. While that might not affect the usefulness of Datext's products, it does point up the need to carefully compare these different products.

There are also opportunities for you to use CD-ROM as a product of your own, both as a consultant helping a company set up its own internal information department and as a publisher of your own CD-ROM database. In the first instance, the CD-ROM would be just another tool a company could use to gather, manage and use information. Just as you might recommend a selection and filing technique for printed journals and a subscription to an online service, you might now recommend the use of a CD-ROM database to a company that has hired you to get their information house in order. Or, if you have developed a database of some limited interest that has not appealed to any of the online database services, it may be possible for you to consider publishing it on CD-ROM. You could even become a value-added reseller of a CD-ROM player and offer your own turnkey information system featuring your own database.

The potential for CD-ROM technology far exceeds the few examples presented in this discussion, but these are some of the characteristics of the technology that appear to have the most interest for the information broker. Within the compact disk industry, there is excited talk about the combination of text, video and audio on one disk, the development of interactive disks and the capabilities of the WORM (Write Once, Read Many times) disks. The first two will encourage very broad educational, recreational, and business use of the technology while the last offers, among other things, the capability of adding proprietary information to a published, public database, thereby creating a much more valuable information product.

In summary, much of the CD-ROM technology still seems to be an answer in search of a question, but as the answer gets better, the sense of urgency about finding the right questions increases. In any event, there's a lot more to CD-ROMs than a more powerful version of the microfiche and a lot less than a total, immediate revolution in the information industry.

CD-ROM in Action: Compact Disclosure

The records found on Compact Disclosure will be immediately familiar to anyone who has used the online Disclosure databases. It is even possible to use DIALOG commands to search Compact Disclosure from the familiar ''?'' prompt, as follows:

COMPACT DISCLOSURE JUL-87 (COPYRIGHT DISCLOSURE)

Set	Items	Description
?		

But most of the searching on the system will be performed in the "Easy Menu Mode." This mode offers several menu options:

Would you like to search by:

Company Name, Ticker or Number
Type of Business
Geographic Area
Annual Financial Information
Quarterly Financial Information

Funds Source/Use Information
Stock Price Information
Ratio Analysis Information
Owners, Officers, Directors
Shares/Employees
Exchange (NYS,AMS,OTH,NMS,NDQ)
Fortune Number

Auditor/Services Information
Management Discussion Text
Pres Letr
Corporate Exhibits Text
Other Corporate Events Text
Financial Comments Text

All Text Fields
Dictionary List
Data in U.S. Currency
Data in Non U.S. Currency
Fiscal Year End (MM/DD)

Selecting the first item on the menu, Company Name, Ticker or Number, brings you to a submenu:

Full Company Name
Words in Company Name
Rotated Company Name
Ticker Symbol
Subsidiary Name
Cross Reference Name
Either Name, Subsidiary or Xref
Disclosure Company Number
D–U–N–S Number

Other selections will produce corresponding submenus until you finally identify the company or companies for which you are searching. The records are identical to those available online (though there may be some differences in the currency of the information), so you'll have no difficulty in working with them. Once your search is concluded, you can choose to save the results or to continue your search:

Display, Print or Transfer the Selected company(s)
Modify the current search with additional criteria
Begin a New Search (clears existing search)
Quit Easy Menu Mode

A simple search on Compact Disclosure for the stock symbol CCI would identify the one company with that stock symbol:

1 of 1 Complete company records
CITICORP
399 PARK AVENUE
NEW YORK NY 10043

TELEPHONE: 212-559-1000
DISCLOSURE CO NO: C375725000
CROSS REFERENCE: WAS FIRST NATIONAL CITY CORP

INCORPORATION: DE
EXCHANGE: NYS
TICKER SYMBOL: CCI

FORTUNE NO: B001
FORBES NO: SA013; AS001; PR020; MV050
CUSIP NO: 0001730340
D-U-N-S NO: 04-525-6872

SIC CODES:
6025 NATIONAL BANKS, FEDERAL RESERVE
6146 Installment Sales Finance Companies
6211 Security Brokers and Dealers

Of course, the record goes on from there, but you get the idea. It's all very familiar, it's all very accessible (without the meter ticking), and it's all very expensive. But while compact disc technology slowly comes down in price, other companies are taking advantage of more affordable technologies to offer the same type of service.

One such company is Corporate Technology Information Services of Wellesley Hills, Mass. This company produces CorpTech, a corporate technology database distributed not on compact disc but on a HardCard, a 20-megabyte hard drive which can be fitted into a slot on most PCs. Using Cosmos, Inc.'s REVELATION database software, this database "contains details on 17,136 firms that develop or manufacture high-tech products in the U.S., or own companies that do so."

This product may not be "state of the art," but it is available now, it is useful (and will continue to be so), and it is more affordable than the same information on CD-ROM would be. It isn't necessary for a "high tech" database to be packaged in the most "high tech" way to be useful. And useful is the key.

Gateway Services

The term "gateway services" can apply to an online bridge between two existing services, such as the one between MCI Mail and Dow Jones News/Retrieval (DJNR) or to a service that provides access to the databases of more than one database vendor, such as EasyNet from Telebase Systems, Inc. Gateway services allow you access to a database service to which you do not subscribe. This can greatly enhance the level of service you can offer your clients, but it can also put you in the middle of something you are not prepared for.

As with all things, it is important to understand what a gateway is designed to do in order to understand what it can do for you. In some cases, as with the MCI Mail/DJNR link, there is little "value added" other than the bi-directional access. In others, such as EasyNet, there is an intermediary computer (and program) that you can use to gain access to the online service. That intermediary computer will often include additional services to make your use of the databases easier. Each type of gateway has its own strengths and weaknesses that must be considered.

Because of its wide availability through a number of online services and as a stand-alone service, Telebase System's EasyNet serves as a good example of these strengths and weaknesses. If you call EasyNet directly, you can gain access to over 850 public databases from vendors such as BRS, Data-Star, DIALOG, NewsNet, ORBIT, VU/TEXT, and H.W. Wilson. Nationally accessible via the standard packet-switching networks (such as Telenet) or an 800 number, EasyNet will charge your search to your credit card. There are no subscription fees, no monthly minimums, no costs other than those related directly to your search. With this ease of access and online human help readily available (just type "SOS" at any prompt), EasyNet can support its claim to be "The Knowledge Gateway."

Not only is EasyNet a gateway service, it is also available on other systems via a gateway. These other services include CompuServe (where the service is called IQuest), Addison-Wesley (EINSTEIN), and Western Union (InfoMaster). These gateways to a gateway are, according to a publicity release from the company, "customized to serve their respective end-user marketplace." In most significant ways, at least, there is no difference between the service you get from EasyNet directly and the service via one of the other gateways. So, for all practical purposes, EasyNet is both a gateway and available through a gateway and will therefore serve as one example for the two types of service.

The availability of EasyNet as a gateway service is proving to be a good marketing decision for Telebase Systems. For example, the day it became available on CompuServe as IQuest, it gained a potential client base of over 375,000 people (the approximate number of subscribers to CompuServe). This was accomplished without the cost or effort of a single direct mail piece or major magazine advertisement. And since it is in CompuServe's best interest to encourage the use of IQuest, they contribute their effort to the marketing of the service. What is true for the relationship with CompuServe is true for Telebase Systems' relationship with every other service on which it is available.

Subscribers to these online services comprise a fairly well targeted market for Telebase Systems, too. They are comfortable with computer telecommunications, they have already established credit accounts with an online system to take care of billing and collection, and in many instances they understand the value (and cost) of information. In return, it is safe to assume that Telebase Systems gives up a portion of the income earned through the use of their service. So long as that portion remains the same or less than the cost of marketing the service directly, the relationship remains a profitable one for all concerned.

Is it a profitable relationship for the person who uses IQuest for a bit of basic online research? We should examine several factors that contribute to the cost of the search in order to answer that question. First, there is the simple matter of the cost of being connected to CompuServe. At 1200 baud, the hourly cost of maintaining a connection to CompuServe is $12.50 which gives a per-minute rate of 20.83 cents. The charges for using IQuest are fairly straightforward. Each time you conduct a search, you are charged a flat fee of $10. If you get no results from your search request, you are generally charged a nominal $1. Some databases carry surcharges (such as Magazine ASAP, a full-text database that carries a $3 surcharge). For your $10, you are shown the first 10 (or, on some databases, 15) citations that result from your search.

At that point, you can end your search and incur no additional charges. If, however, you want more citations, you are charged an additional $10 for every 10 or 15 you retrieve. If, on the other hand, you are happy with the citations and want to see the abstracts or full-text articles, you can do that, too, for an additional charge.

Assuming the searcher retrieved 20 citations from a database with no search surcharge and then asked for abstracts for five of those citations and spent 10 minutes conducting the search and retrieving the information, the costs would be:

10 minutes on CompuServe	$ 2.09
1 database search	10.00
10 additional citations	10.00
5 abstracts (@$2.00)	10.00
Total Cost	$32.09

Suppose, however, the search required more information. Say it covered three different databases, one full-text, and took 30 minutes. And assume that from the full-text database, two articles were retrieved (the first one was free) from 15 citations and from each of the other two databases, four abstracts were chosen from 30 citations. In that event, the costs would be:

30 minutes on CompuServe	$ 6.25
3 search requests	33.00
40 additional citations	40.00
8 abstracts	16.00
2 full-text articles (1 free)	15.00
Total Cost	$110.25

While online costs in any environment can add up very quickly, it takes only a simple extension of this cost estimating to show that a system such as EasyNet is best suited for quick, precisely focused searches. And, while all searches must be precisely focused, if you expect a large number of citations to result from your search and you expect to have an interest in many of them, the EasyNet costs can add up very quickly. In that instance, direct access to the database would have to be the preferred method.

The value to an information broker of a system like EasyNet comes when it gives you access to a system you would not otherwise be able to use, especially when that system would cost you a monthly service or minimum usage charge. Unless you make extensive use of such a system, it isn't worth it to pay these minimum fees. In the case of EasyNet, an example would be the access it gives to NewsNet, a database of newsletters. NewsNet charges a monthly subscription of $15. This is not a tremendous amount of money, but in any business it pays to save $180 per year where you can. Of course, if you're going to make extensive use of NewsNet, it makes good sense to subscribe. If, however, you plan to make only sporadic use of the service, EasyNet might be a better choice.

EasyNet also can serve as an easy way to demonstrate the power of online searching to your clients. With a portable computer and modem, you can offer an on-the-spot demonstration of a simple online search right in the client's office. Because EasyNet offers the service both as menu-driven and as command driven, you can run the search without lugging about the DIALOG Bluesheets. You can pick the appropriate database, if you know it, or you can allow EasyNet to choose the database. By being able to provide an ''instant answer'' to a hypothetical question posed by the client during the interview, you can clearly demonstrate the power of online information. Just make sure the demo doesn't give the client all of the information he needs, or you've lost a sale.

Gateways do have drawbacks, however. Let's look at the weaknesses inherent in them and consider how they would limit the system's value to an information broker.

Perhaps the most glaring weakness of gateway systems is the limited power they allow the user. Many of the more sophisticated search techniques available when accessing a database directly are not available through a gateway service. On EasyNet, there are several examples of this. On NewsNet, you can search all of the newsletters or a single newsletter or a pre-defined group of newsletters at one time, or you can define your own select group of newsletters. Via EasyNet, you can search only an individual newsletter or one of the predefined groups of newsletters. While any search of the full database of newsletters available on NewsNet is a very time-consuming process and may, thus, be of little value, the ability to specify two or more specific newsletters to be searched is valuable.

To search five newsletters via EasyNet, it would be necessary to search them one at a time. At a minimum of $10 per search, it would cost $50 just to run your search query in each of the newsletters. For additional citations or full-text articles, the cost would increase. Also, NewsNet offers a ''current awareness'' or electronic clipping service called NewsFlash. This service is not available via EasyNet. Again, however, if you're going to make extensive use of the NewsNet databases, you'll want to access them directly.

In the case of a DIALOG search, EasyNet does not offer access to the DIALIN-DEX database (File 411). This database, while limited, does allow you to make good decisions about which databases to search. On EasyNet, your only assistance in selecting a database is that offered by the menus in EasyNet I (We Pick the Database). While you have an alternative (EasyNet II—You Pick the Database), there is no DIALINDEX-type help offered in selecting the database. Complex search terms also are harder to use on EasyNet. With direct access to DIALOG, you can build as complex a search request as your abilities will allow. And once the results of that search request are available, you can modify and/or build on that request to further refine your search. With EasyNet, you must either stick with the results of your search or back out and start over with a new search. And finally, tools such as the EXPAND command, which helps you choose the right search term, are not currently available through EasyNet.

There are two versions of EasyNet available online (EasyNet I and EasyNet II). These versions are distinct enough that you should know their similarities and differences. EasyNet I will choose the database to be searched based on your selections from a series of menus. First, you define the nature of your question and the topic of your question. Then you select the source of the information you are seeking. Finally, either EasyNet makes the selection for you or presents you with a short list of databases and asks you to make the selection. In a trial use of the system, the EasyNet I service seemed to take many trails to just a few databases. It is probably not possible for any workable menu system to provide full access to over 850 public databases, and the system apparently selects the most widely applicable ones for inclusion in this system. The assumption may be that if you really need to use the Biotechnology Investment Opportunities database, you'll know to ask for it directly from EasyNet II.

This weakness of the EasyNet service does not mean the service is worthless. It has, as has been stated, very definite uses just as it has very definite areas in which it is of limited usefulness. You need to know what the system does and, more importantly, what it attempts to do, in order to know what it can do for you. Clearly, the system is designed to be useful to a large number of people, many of whom have absolutely no experience or training in searching an online database. It is designed to provide information in small bites to help control the cost of that information. And it is designed to be as widely available as possible so that it might become, at least sometimes, the first choice of someone who is looking for answers.

On the other side of this question, the system is not designed to satisfy all of the online research needs of a serious, professional online searcher. While its EasyNet II service does allow a little more power than EasyNet I, it does not offer the full power and capabilities of the online database services themselves. Therefore, for the information broker, EasyNet might fill in a gap or two, particularly in providing access to databases to which the broker would not otherwise subscribe. But it will not serve the professional's information needs in any but the most modest circumstances.

Searching the Gateway: Online with EasyNet

In order to demonstrate the way EasyNet works, and to exhibit some of its strengths and weaknesses, a simple search will be recorded here. The only editing of this search transcript has been done to conserve space, remove control characters and confidential information, and increase readability. The purpose of this search was to find out what has been written recently about think tanks that deal with religion or religious matters. The transcript of the search will be in the right-hand column; the left-hand column will be used for explanatory comments. Instructions and other items typed in by the searcher will appear in **bold** type.

```
                    ** EASYNET **
                 The Knowledge Gateway
                  ** ANNOUNCEMENTS **
     PRICING CHANGE EFFECTIVE 9/1/87.
     $10 per search, telecom .35 per min.
     See News off Main Menu for details.
     To protect users from credit fraud,
     we will require a signed application
     form. As of Sept. 1, instant access
     will not be possible until the form
     is submitted.
     Please enter your Visa, Mastercard,
     American Express or EasyNet Account
     number.
     Type L to leave EasyNet.
     ->
     Card Holder's Name:
     ->

     Is this correct? (Yes/No) -> y
     +------------------------------------+
     |                                    |
     |          WELCOME TO EASYNET        |
     |          (c) 1987 Pat. Pend.       |
     |         Telebase Systems Inc.      |
     |            Customer Service        |
     |            1-800-841-9553          |
     |           (in PA 215-526-2835)     |
     |                                    |
     +------------------------------------+


     Logon 1104167 16SEP87 23:55 EST
```

This is the top menu which gives you the choice between a menu-driven system and a command system. You'll see it frequently.

```
     PRESS TO SELECT
      1 EasyNet-I We pick the database
      2 EasyNet-II You pick the database
      3 Database Directory
      4 News, Instructions
      H Help
     Total charges thus far: $0.35
     -> 1
```

Having chosen the menu-driven system, you are now asked to begin to define your search topic.

```
     PRESS TO SELECT
      1 Subject
      2 Person
      3 Place
      4 Organization
      H Help
     Total charges thus far: $0.35
     -> 1
```

Yours is a subject search, and you are given this menu so that you can refine the subject focus of your search. Your selection is religion and philosophy.

```
PRESS TO SELECT
 1 Current Events
 2 Business, Economics
 3 Computers, Sci/Tech, Medicine
 4 Law, Trademarks, Patents
 5 Social Sciences, Education
 6 Art, Literature, Entertainment
 7 Religion, Philosophy
 H Help
Total charges thus far: $0.35
-> 7
```

Asked to choose between the two, your selection is religion.

```
PRESS TO SELECT
 1 Religion
 2 Philosophy
 H Help
Total charges thus far: $0.35
-> 1
```

While these terms are not too clearly defined, you elect to try to find what you're looking for in general periodicals which shouldn't carry more in-depth articles than the lay-person could understand.

```
PRESS TO SELECT
 1 Scholarly journals
 2 General periodicals
 3 Popular magazines
 4 Books on religion
 5 Encyclopedias
 6 List of related databases
 H Help
Total charges thus far: $0.35
-> 2
```

```
Enter your specific topic.
(type H for important examples or B to back up)
-> h
```

Before choosing your specific search term, you decide to take a look at the help offered by the system. You want to know what tools are available to you in phrasing your search request.

```
CONNECTING WORDS
 Don't use small words like:
     by, from, in, of, the, at
 EX: Joan Arc instead of
     Joan of Arc.
WILD LETTERS
 Use / as a 'wild letter' at the
     end of a word.
 EX: democ/ will retrieve democracy
         democratic
         Democrats
   Tax/ will retrieve tax
         taxes
         taxation
LOGIC WORDS (and, or, not)
     Use  AND   to find items common
```

```
         to two or more subjects.
EX: dog AND leash
    police AND civilian control
    debt AND management


Press (return) to continue...->

  Use  OR  to find items on
       either or both subjects.
  EX: Bach OR Handel
      dog OR cat OR pet
  Use   NOT  to exclude a
        subject from another.
  EX: candy NOT taffy
      housing NOT mobile homes
  Use  (  )  around groups.
  EX: (dog OR cat OR pet) AND leash
      eskimo/ AND (lawyer/ or attorn/)
Press (return) to continue...->

Enter your specific topic.
(type H for important examples or B to back up)

-> think tank/

Is:
THINK TANK/
 Correct ? (Yes/No) -> y
```

Since there does not appear to be any way to select a phrase search, you elect to use "think tank/" as your search term, hoping the system will know the difference between the phrase you use and the words think and tank/, which you did not want to use. The system chooses the Humanities Index for your search.

```
System is searching the Humanities Index database,
copyrighted 1987 by H. W. Wilson Company, New York, NY and
available through Wilsonline. We have no reason to believe
that errors exist in the data or services furnished. If
there are any such errors the parties hereto have no
liability for any consequential, incidental or punitive
damages. No warranty, either expressed or implied,
including but not limited to those of merchantability or
fitness for a particular purpose are made. Any liability is
limited to the amount paid by the customer to EasyNet.


Accessing Network..........Connected.
Accessing Database Vendor...Unable to complete database
                search.
Trying again, lines may be Unavailable.
Accessing Network..........Connected.
Accessing Database Vendor...Unable to complete database
                search.
Try Again? (Yes/No) -> n

Please wait...
```

For some reason, the system is unable to complete your search and you don't know how to proceed. You decide to ask for human help, using the SOS feature of the system.

```
PRESS  TO SELECT
 1 Search same database
 2 Search different database
Total charges thus far:  $2.10
-> sos


Please wait...


Accessing SOS facility...Completed.
You are now in direct communications with an SOS staff
member.
Please respond when you see the    ->
When you want to leave SOS, and return to the
search system, type  BYE   on a separate line.

HI THIS IS KATE. HOW CAN I HELP YOU?

-> I was trying to find articles about religious think
tanks but the database I was trying to use isn't available.

-> I'M ALSO HELPING ANOTHER PERSON. MY RESPONSES MAY BE
SLOW. PLEASE BEAR WITH ME!

-> ok!

-> WHICH MESSAGE DID YOU RECEIVE WHEN YOU TRIED TO ACCESS
THAT DATABASE??

-> I got a "connected" message with the Network but no
access to the specific database. The System tried twice,
but no luck.

-> OH , THERE ARE CERTAIN HOURS WHEN THE VENDORS ARE DOWN
... YOU MIGHT TRY ANOTHER DATABASE ... RELIGION INDEX OR
PHILOSOPHERS INDEX

-> OK, I'll give that a try. One more question. Is it
possible to use any kind of proximity indicator in the
search (as the (w) indicator)?

-> YES, YOU CAN USE THE BOOLEAN TERMS   AND  OR
...HOWEVER, THEY NEED TO BE USED CAREFULLY ... SUGGEST YOU
LOOK AT HELP SCREENS FOR THEIR USE ... ALSO, IT DOES DEPEND
ON THE VENDOR AS TO HOW COMPLEX A SEARCH YOU CAN
FORMULATE...

-> I've tried the help screens (and have been helped), but
have seen no suggestion about how to search on a specific
phrase (such as "think tank"). What I'd like to do is
something like (think(w1)tank/) and religio/. Is there any
way to do that?
```

E

-> YES, AND YOU HAVE PRETTY MUCH DONE IT ... YOU DO NOT
NEED THE PARENTHESES WHEN THE WORDS ARE PART OF THE SAME
PHRASE... YOU COULD SAY: THINK TANK/ AND RELIGIO/   WHERAS
YOU WOULD NEED THEM TO ASK FOR   (THINK TANK/ OR SEMINAR/)
AND RELIGIO/

-> **I see. So the use of the phrase think tank/ absent any
parentheses or quotations or anything else implies the
phrase "think tank/" rather than the words "think" and
"tank/"?**

-> YES IN NEARLY ALL VENDORS ... THERE ARE A COUPLE OF
EXCEPTIONS WHERE YOU MIGHT BE SEARCHING NEWSPAPERS, ETC ..
BUT FOR THE INDEXES I THINK YOU UNDERSTAND HOW IT WORKS

-> **OK, I'll give it a try and, if it doesn't work, I'll
just SOS again.**

-> **bye**

Please wait...

PRESS TO SELECT
 1 Search same database
 2 Search different database
Total charges thus far: $7.35
-> 2

PRESS TO SELECT
 1 EasyNet-I We pick the database
 2 EasyNet-II You pick the database
 3 Database Directory
 4 News, Instructions
 H Help
Total charges thus far: $7.35
-> 2

Please enter the database name as you know it
(use B to back up)
Total charges thus far: $7.35
-> **religion index**
Searching...

PRESS TO SELECT
 1 basic searching
 2 field searching
 H Help
Total charges thus far: $7.35
-> h

You take the advice of the EasyNet employee and decide to search Religion Index. Since you know the name of this database, you can return to the top menu and select EasyNet-II where you can pick the database to be searched.

Once the system identifies the database you have chosen, you are taken directly to it with no other intervening menus.

You notice that basic and field searching are available here, so you ask about the specifics.

If you chose a field, it would be the subject field anyway, so you choose basic searching.

Before deciding on your search term, you again want to see what tools are available to you here to help refine your search request.

BASIC SEARCHING: enables you to search by subject.
FIELD SEARCHING: enables you to search by subject, author, reviewer, and/or publication year.

Press (return) to continue...->

PRESS TO SELECT
 1 basic searching
 2 field searching
 H Help
Total charges thus far: $7.35
-> 1

Enter your religion topic (e.g., SALVATION; ILLUSION/ AND REALIT/).

Type H for Search Guidelines.
(or type B to back up)
-> h

```
=======================================
            TOPIC SEARCH GUIDE
=======================================
```
COMBINED TERMS: Use AND to search ALL of the terms entered, OR to search ANY of the terms entered:
    Mecca AND pilgrimage
    Savior OR Messiah
GROUPS: Group related terms in PARENTHESES, separated by OR:
    (prayer OR faith) AND healing
Press (return) to continue...->

WILD LETTERS: Use the WILD LETTER slash (/) to search variable word endings:
USE: Christ/
TO GET: Christ, Christ's, Christian, Christianity, etc.
PUNCTUATION: Omit all. Enter hyphenated terms with and without a space with OR; enter other punctuated words as single terms:
USE: Neo Platonism OR Neoplatonism
FOR: Neo-Platonism
USE: CYO FOR: C.Y.O or C Y O
USE: Chan FOR: Ch'an
Press (return) to continue...->

Once again, phrase searching does not seem possible, so you use "and" to connect the two components of your search request. There's a common search error in this request. Can you spot it?

In this case, you successfully log on to the database and begin the search.

The system returns to inform you of your very basic search error. You asked to search RELIGIO/ in the Religion Index database. That is far too common a term.

```
              * PERSONAL NAMES *
ENTRY METHOD: Enter the last name only;
combine with subject words using AND:
         Neibuhr AND freedom
         * ORGANIZATIONAL NAMES *
ENTRY METHOD:  Enter abbreviated and
full forms, separated by OR; omit words
such as Company, Corp., Inc., etc.:
     WCC OR World Council Churches
Press (return) to continue...->


Enter your religion topic (e.g., SALVATION; ILLUSION/ AND
REALIT/).
Type H for Search Guidelines.
(or type B to back up)
-> (think tank/) and religio/


Is:
(THINK TANK/) AND RELIGIO/
 Correct ? (Yes/No) -> y


System is now searching the Religion Index database,
copyrighted 1987 by the American Theological Library
Association, Chicago, IL and available through BRS
Information Technologies.

Accessing network..........Connected.
Accessing Database Vendor...Completed.
Logging on..................Completed.
Logging on (second step)....Completed.
Selecting Database..........Completed.

Each star equals one line of retrieved data. This may take
several minutes...

Your search is too general. Enter specific terms in place
of the WILD LETTER slash (/) (e.g., USE: (music OR musical
OR musically) FOR: music/).
Nothing was retrieved. No charge for this search.

Press (return) to continue...->

Please wait...

PRESS  TO SELECT
 1 Search same database
 2 Search different database
Total charges thus far: $8.05
-> 1
```

```
PRESS  TO SELECT
 1 basic searching
 2 field searching
 H Help
Total charges thus far: $8.05
-> 1
```

```
Enter your religion topic (e.g., SALVATION; ILLUSION/ AND
REALIT/).
Type H for Search Guidelines.
(or type B to back up)
```

So you decide to eliminate that term from your search request and try again.

```
-> think tank/
```

```
Is:
THINK TANK/
 Correct ? (Yes/No) -> y
```

```
System is now searching the Religion Index database,
copyrighted 1987 by the American Theological Library
Association, Chicago, IL and available through BRS
Information Technologies.
```

```
Accessing network..........Connected.
Accessing Database Vendor...Completed.
Logging on.................Completed.
Logging on (second step)....Completed.
Selecting Database.........Completed.
```

This time your results are better and, after a bit, the system returns to give you the results of your search. If there had been more than 10 items satisfying the search phrase, you would have been shown only the most recent 10 (in some databases, the most recent 15).

```
Each star equals one line of retrieved data. This may take
several minutes...
```

```
**************************************************
***************************
```

```
Search completed...........
```

```
There are 5 item(s) which
satisfy your search phrase.
You may wish to PRINT or CAPTURE this data if possible.
```

```
Press (return) to see your search results...->
```

```
Heading # 1                    Searched: Sep 17, 1987  0:20
Use (^S) to stop; (^Q) to resume; (^O) to advance; (^C) to
interrupt.
AN 601119. (RD). 8612.
AU KETCHAM-DONALD-H-DMIN.
TI MINISTRY WITH BUSINESS PERSONS IN THE LOCAL CHURCH.
SO HARTFORD SEMINARY, 1986, 200+PP.
YR 86.
Press (return) to continue...->
```

```
Heading # 2
AN 280816. (RI). 8606.
AU LADIPO-YEMI.
TI DO WE NEED A CHRISTIAN THINK TANK CONFERENCE IN AFRICA.
SO E AFRICA J EV TH. 3 NO 1,4-15 1984.
YR 84.
Press (return) to continue...->


Heading # 3
AN 279113. (RI). 8604.
AU ROBINSON-JAMES-M.
TI HOW MY MIND HAS CHANGED (OR REMAINED THE SAME)
(BIBLIOG).
SO S B L SEM PAP. NO 24,481-504 1985.
YR 85.
Press (return) to continue...->


Heading # 4
AN 264227. (RI). 8505.
AU HENRY-CARL-F-H.
TI WHY WE NEED CHRISTIAN THINK TANKS (INTERVIEW EDITORIAL).
SO CHR T. 29 NO 5,14-15 MR 15 1985.
YR 85.


Press (return) to continue...->


Heading # 5
AN 002478. (RI). 0000.
AU THOMPSON-NORMA-H.
TI FUTURISM: ITS IMPLICATIONS FOR RELIGIOUS EDUCATION.
SO ST LUKE J. 18,150-174. MR 75.
YR 75.
Press (return) to continue...->

PRESS    TO SELECT
  1  Review results again
  3  Order reprints
  5  Start a new search
  6  Leave System
Total charges thus far:  $18.75
-> 5
Please wait...

PRESS    TO SELECT
  1 Search same database
  2 Search different database
Total charges thus far:  $19.10
-> 2
```

Had there been more than the minimum number of hits, another menu item (2) would have been presented to you: *See additional items*. There would be an additional charge for that service.

Being satisfied with your search results, you leave Religion Index.

Now see what the general press might have to say on the matter. At the top menu, you select Easy-Net-I.

```
PRESS   TO SELECT
 1 EasyNet-I  We pick the database
 2 EasyNet-II You pick the database
 3 Database Directory
 4 News, Instructions
 H Help
Total charges thus far:  $19.10
-> 1
```

```
PRESS   TO SELECT
 1 Subject
 2 Person
 3 Place
 4 Organization
 H Help
Total charges thus far:  $19.10
-> 1
```

This time your interest is in current events rather than religion.

```
PRESS   TO SELECT
 1 Current Events
 2 Business, Economics
 3 Computers, Sci/Tech, Medicine
 4 Law, Trademarks, Patents
 5 Social Sciences, Education
 6 Art, Literature, Entertainment
 7 Religion, Philosophy
 H Help
Total charges thus far:  $19.10
-> 1
```

```
PRESS   TO SELECT
 1 International Newspapers
 2 Regional Newspapers
 3 International Wire Services
 H Help
Total charges thus far:  $19.10
-> 1
```

Obviously, the Monitor is an interesting option, but the full-text of the Washington Post is too tempting.

```
PRESS   TO SELECT
 1 Christian Science Monitor (bibl)
 2 Financial Times (text)
 3 New York Times (bibl)
 4 Wall Street Journal (bibl)
 5 Washington Post (text)
 H Help
Total charges thus far:  $19.10
-> 5
```

Your interest is in what might have been written recently, so your obvious choice is the current file.

```
PRESS  TO SELECT
 1 Washington Post          Current file (1987)
 2 Washington Post           Back file  (1986)
 3 Washington Post           Back file  (1985)
 4 Washington Post           Back file  (1984)
 5 Washington Post           Back file  (1983)
 H Help
Total charges thus far:  $19.10
-> 1
```

Again you are offered basic or field searching, but, remembering your experience with Religion Index, your choice is basic searching.

```
PRESS  TO SELECT
 1 basic searching
 2 field searching
 H Help
Total charges thus far:  $19.10
-> 1
```

```
Enter your specific topic (e.g., SENATE AND IMMIGRA/).
NOTE: Do not search with PARENTHESES or PUNCTUATION in this
database. Type H for IMPORTANT Search Guidelines.
(or type B to back up)
```

The broader nature of this database will require the use of religio/ as part of your search term.

```
-> think tank/ and religio/

Is:
THINK TANK/ AND RELIGIO/
 Correct ? (Yes/No) -> y
```

```
System is now searching the Washington Post database,
copyrighted 1987 by the Washington Post, Washington, DC and
available through VU/TEXT Information Services, Inc.
```

```
Accessing Network..........Connected.
Accessing Database Vendor...Completed.
Logging on.................Unable to complete database
                    search.
```

Unfortunately, it seems as though, once again, you've chosen a database that is not currently available.

```
Trying again, lines may be Unavailable.
Accessing Network..........Connected.
Accessing Database Vendor...Completed.
Logging on.................Unable to complete database
                    search.
Try Again? (Yes/No) -> n
```

```
Please wait...
```

```
PRESS  TO SELECT
 1 Search same database
 2 Search different database
Total charges thus far:  $20.50
-> 2
```

So it's back to the top menu to try again.

```
PRESS  TO SELECT
 1 EasyNet-I  We pick the database
 2 EasyNet-II You pick the database
 3 Database Directory
 4 News, Instructions
 H Help
Total charges thus far:  $20.50
-> 1

PRESS  TO SELECT
 1 Subject
 2 Person
 3 Place
 4 Organization
 H Help
Total charges thus far:  $20.50
-> 1

PRESS  TO SELECT
 1 Current Events
 2 Business, Economics
 3 Computers, Sci/Tech, Medicine
 4 Law, Trademarks, Patents
 5 Social Sciences, Education
 6 Art, Literature, Entertainment
 7 Religion, Philosophy
 H Help
Total charges thus far:  $20.50
-> 1

PRESS   TO SELECT
 1 International Newspapers
 2 Regional Newspapers
 3 International Wire Services
 H Help
Total charges thus far:  $20.50
-> 1
```

This time you opt for the authority of the New York Times, even if it is only in bibliographic form.

```
PRESS  TO SELECT
 1 Christian Science Monitor (bibl)
 2 Financial Times (text)
 3 New York Times (bibl)
 4 Wall Street Journal (bibl)
 5 Washington Post (text)
 H Help
Total charges thus far:  $20.50
-> 3
```

Again, your obvious choice is the current file.

```
PRESS  TO SELECT
 1 Current file(approx last 45 days)
 2 Back file   (1987)
 3 Back file   (1986)
 4 Back file   (1985)
 5 Back file   (1984)
 6 Back file   (1979 - 1983)
 H Help
Total charges thus far: $20.85
-> 2


Enter your specific topic.
(type H for important examples or B to back up)

-> (think tank/) and religio/


Is:
(THINK TANK/) AND RELIGIO/
 Correct ? (Yes/No) -> y
```

You notice that although you chose the New York Times as the source, the System is using the National Newspaper Index. Obviously, the system is including a limitation on your search to confine it to the Times.

```
System is now searching the National Newspaper Index
database, copyrighted 1987 by Information Access Company,
Belmont, CA and available through Dialog Information
Services, Inc.

Accessing network...........Connected.
Accessing Database Vendor...Completed.
Logging on.................Completed.
Logging on (second step)....Completed.
Selecting Database.........Completed.

Each star equals one line of retrieved data. This may take
several minutes...

Occurrence Search expression
---------- -----------------
      762 THINK
     1843 TANK/
       82 THINK TANK/
     7429 RELIGIO/
   662027 NEW YORK TIMES
    85754 1987
        0 Combined expressions
```

Since your search produced no results, you are shown the number of occurrences of each search term and asked for instructions.

```
Nothing was retrieved.
$1 charge for this search.
Press (return) to continue...->

Please wait...
```

Not quite ready to abandon the search, you ask to search another database and are returned to the top menu.

```
PRESS  TO SELECT
 1 Search same database
 2 Search different database
Total charges thus far:  $22.20
-> 2

PRESS  TO SELECT
 1 EasyNet-I  We pick the database
 2 EasyNet-II You pick the database
 3 Database Directory
 4 News, Instructions
 H Help
Total charges thus far:  $22.55
-> 1

PRESS  TO SELECT
 1 Subject
 2 Person
 3 Place
 4 Organization
 H Help
Total charges thus far:  $22.55
-> 1

PRESS  TO SELECT
 1 Current Events
 2 Business, Economics
 3 Computers, Sci/Tech, Medicine
 4 Law, Trademarks, Patents
 5 Social Sciences, Education
 6 Art, Literature, Entertainment
 7 Religion, Philosophy
 H Help
Total charges thus far:  $22.55
-> 1

PRESS  TO SELECT
 1 International Newspapers
 2 Regional Newspapers
 3 International Wire Services
 H Help
Total charges thus far:  $22.55
-> 1
```

This time you give in to your initial impulse and choose to search the Christian Science Monitor.

```
PRESS  TO SELECT
 1 Christian Science Monitor (bibl)
 2 Financial Times (text)
 3 New York Times (bibl)
 4 Wall Street Journal (bibl)
 5 Washington Post (text)
 H Help
Total charges thus far:  $22.55
-> 1
```

This time the current file may be too current, so you select the 1987 back file.

```
PRESS  TO SELECT
 1 Current file(approx last 45 days)
 2 Back file  (1987)
 3 Back file  (1986)
 4 Back file  (1985)
 5 Back file  (1984)
 6 Back file  (1979 - 1983)
 H Help
Total charges thus far:  $22.55
-> 2
```

You decide to risk including religio/ in your search term.

```
Enter your specific topic.
(type H for important examples or B to back up)

-> (think tank/) and religio/

Is:
(THINK TANK/) AND RELIGIO/
 Correct ? (Yes/No) -> y
```

You notice that, again, you are taken into the National Newspaper Index. One paper at a time.

```
System is now searching the National Newspaper Index
database, copyrighted 1987 by Information Access Company,
Belmont, CA and available through Dialog Information
Services, Inc.

Accessing network...........Connected.
Accessing Database Vendor...Completed.
Logging on..................Completed.
Logging on (second step)....Completed.
Selecting Database..........Completed.
```

Again, your search is fruitless, but at least you can see how the system is structuring your search. It seems that "think tank/" is being treated as a phrase and the system is limiting the scope of the search to one publication.

```
Each star equals one line of retrieved data. This may take
several minutes...

Occurrence Search expression
---------- ------------------
    762 THINK
   1843 TANK/
     82 THINK TANK/
   7429 RELIGIO/
  96974 CHRISTIAN SCIENCE MONITOR
  85754 1987
      0 Combined expressions


Nothing was retrieved.
$1 charge for this search.
Press (return) to continue...->

Please wait...
```

PRESS TO SELECT
 1 Search same database
 2 Search different database
Total charges thus far: $24.25
-> 2

PRESS TO SELECT
 1 EasyNet-I We pick the database
 2 EasyNet-II You pick the database
 3 Database Directory
 4 News, Instructions
 H Help
Total charges thus far: $24.25
-> 2

Please enter the database name as you know it
(use B to back up)
Total charges thus far: $24.25

-> national newspaper index

Searching........................

PRESS TO SELECT
 1 basic searching
 2 field searching
 H Help
Total charges thus far: $24.25
-> 1

Enter your specific topic. DO NOT USE HYPHENS (for example:
Mason Dixon Line). Type H for IMPORTANT search guidelines
and examples.
(or type B to back up)

-> (think tank/) and religio/

Is:
(THINK TANK/) AND RELIGIO/
 Correct ? (Yes/No) -> y

PRESS TO SELECT
 1   Start the search
 2   Add more fields
-> 1

System is searching the National Newspaper Index database,
copyrighted 1987 by Information Access Company, Belmont, CA
and available through Dialog Information Services, Inc.

Having been frustrated by the piecemeal approach to searching the National Newspaper Index, you try a different approach: choosing to search the entire database at one time.

Here's a new option: Add more fields. But, you have no more fields and choose to begin the search.

```
Accessing network..........Connected.
Accessing Database Vendor...Completed.
Logging on.................Completed.
Logging on (second step)....Completed.
Selecting Database.........Completed.
```

Once again, your search request produces no results, but at least this time it tried all of the newspapers included in the database. And, the cost of trying wasn't too steep.

```
Each star equals one line of retrieved data. This may take
several minutes...

Occurrence Search expression
---------- ------------------
     762 THINK
    1843 TANK/
      82 THINK TANK/
    7429 RELIGIO/
       0 Combined expressions


Nothing was retrieved.
$1 charge for this search.

Press (return) to continue...->

Please wait...

PRESS  TO SELECT
 1 Search same database
 2 Search different database.
Total charges thus far:  $25.60
-> 2
```

Before you leave, you want to make just one more effort at finding another article or two on your topic.

```
PRESS   TO SELECT
 1 EasyNet-I  We pick the database
 2 EasyNet-II You pick the database
 3 Database Directory
 4 News, Instructions
 H Help
Total charges thus far:  $25.60
-> 1

PRESS   TO SELECT
 1 Subject
 2 Person
 3 Place
 4 Organization
 H Help
Total charges thus far:  $25.60
-> 1
```

You start to try Current Events again, but the next menu reminds you of where you'll end up, so you use the back up option to go a different direction.

```
PRESS  TO SELECT
 1 Current Events
 2 Business, Economics
 3 Computers, Sci/Tech, Medicine
 4 Law, Trademarks, Patents
 5 Social Sciences, Education
 6 Art, Literature, Entertainment
 7 Religion, Philosophy
 H Help
Total charges thus far:  $25.60
-> 1

PRESS  TO SELECT
 1 International Newspapers
 2 Regional Newspapers
 3 International Wire Services
 H Help
Total charges thus far:  $25.60
-> b
```

Your success so far was in the religion database, so you decide to try that area again.

```
PRESS  TO SELECT
 1 Current Events
 2 Business, Economics
 3 Computers, Sci/Tech, Medicine
 4 Law, Trademarks, Patents
 5 Social Sciences, Education
 6 Art, Literature, Entertainment
 7 Religion, Philosophy
 H Help
Total charges thus far:  $25.60
-> 7

PRESS  TO SELECT
 1 Religion
 2 Philosophy
 H Help
Total charges thus far:  $25.95
-> 1
```

Rather than general periodicals, you decide to try popular magazines this time (but can you clearly define the difference?).

```
PRESS  TO SELECT
 1 Scholarly journals
 2 General periodicals
 3 Popular magazines
 4 Books on religion
 5 Encyclopedias
 6 List of related databases
 H Help
Total charges thus far:  $25.95
-> 3
```

From this menu, you deduce that you are given a choice between Magazine Index and Magazine ASAP. Wanting broad coverage, you select Magazine Index.

```
PRESS  TO SELECT
 1 Bibliography (references only)  (1.5 million from
                      435 magazines)
 2 Full-text article  (10 thousand from 50 magazines)
 H Help
Total charges thus far:  $25.95
-> 1

Enter your specific topic (e.g., INVESTMENT/; UNIONS AND
POLITICAL ).
Type H for Search Guidelines.
(or type B to back up)

-> (think tank/) and religio/

Is:
(THINK TANK/) AND RELIGIO/
 Correct ? (Yes/No) -> y

System is searching the Magazine Index database,
copyrighted 1987 by Information Access Company, Belmont, CA
and available through BRS Information Technologies.

Accessing network...........Connected.
Accessing Database Vendor...Completed.
Logging on.................Completed.
Logging on (second step)....Completed.
Selecting Database.........Completed.

Each star equals one line of retrieved data. This may take
several minutes...
```

However, you are once again foiled in your effort.

```
Nothing was retrieved.
$1 charge for this search.

Press (return) to continue...->

Please wait...

PRESS  TO SELECT
 1 Search same database
 2 Search different database
Total charges thus far:  $27.30
-> 1
```

If Magazine Index doesn't have it, maybe Magazine ASAP, with the ability to search the full text of the article, might.

```
PRESS  TO SELECT
 1 Bibliography (references only)  (1.5 million from
                      435 magazines)
 2 Full-text article (10 thousand from 50 magazines)
 H Help
Total charges thus far:  $27.65
-> 2
```

Searching a full-text database costs a little more, but you're worth it.

This database carries a surcharge of $ 3 for this search.
Do you wish to continue ? (Yes/No) -> **y**

Enter your specific topic (e.g., INVESTMENT/; UNIONS AND POLITICAL).
Type H for Search Guidelines.
(or type B to back up)

-> **(think tank/) and religio/**

Is:
(THINK TANK/) AND RELIGIO/
 Correct ? (Yes/No) -> **y**

System is searching the Magazine ASAP database, copyrighted 1987 by Information Access Company, Belmont, CA and available through BRS Information Technologies.

Accessing network..........Connected.
Accessing Database Vendor...Completed.
Logging on................Completed.
Logging on (second step)....Completed.
Selecting Database.........Completed.

Each star equals one line of retrieved data. This may take several minutes...
Nothing was retrieved.
$1 charge for this search.

Press (return) to continue...->

Please wait...

OK, you're convinced. You're not going to find anything else on this topic. You want out.

PRESS TO SELECT
 1 Search same database
 2 Search different database
Total charges thus far: $29.00
-> **b**

But before you leave, you're curious about the options available from the top menu, in case there's something you've overlooked.

PRESS TO SELECT
 1 EasyNet-I We pick the database
 2 EasyNet-II You pick the database
 3 Database Directory
 4 News, Instructions
 H Help
Total charges thus far: $29.00
-> **h**

EasyNet-I: When you don't have a specific database in mind. Select your categories and follow the menus to the type of information you seek. Lists of related databases are also provided. Enter your search terms at the appropriate prompt, and the system will convert them into the vendor's command language. The cost of each search is fixed.

EasyNet-II: Has a greater selection of databases. Type in the database name and enter your search terms. These are translated into the command language of the vendor. The cost of each search is fixed.

Database Directory: Provides names and descriptions of databases accessed by EasyNet. You may search by subject category, database name, or keywords from the name. There is no charge for this service. ** NOTE: some of the databases listed may not be available on this service at this time. **

You read about the options available to you from this menu and see nothing that might help reverse the results you've been getting.

Press (return) to continue...->

```
     FIVE BASIC COMMANDS
  H = Help
  B = Back up one frame
  M = Return to Main menu
SOS = Online human assistance
  L = Leave EasyNet
```

You've used the help and the SOS option to ask for help, without much success. The only option that appeals to you now is Leave EasyNet.

Press (return) to continue...->

```
PRESS  TO SELECT
 1 EasyNet-I  We pick the database
 2 EasyNet-II You pick the database
 3 Database Directory
 4 News, Instructions
 H Help
Total charges thus far:  $29.00
-> 1
```

On your way out, you're given a nice summary of the money you've spent in your search.

```
          Charges:
System Access:
   Telecommunications    $14.35
Database Charges:
  1 Searches:           $10.00
  6 No-hit Searches:     $5.00
  0 Reprints:            $0.00
  0 Express Reprints:    $0.00
  0 Abstracts           $0.00
    Surcharges          $0.00
  Total Charges:       $29.35
```

Logoff 1104167 17SEP87 0:36 EST
    Thank you for calling!

Gateway Software

Essential to your work as an information broker is a telecommunications program. Even if you plan to make only minimal use of online database services, when you do use them, you will need software in order to get your computer to call the other computer and put the question to it.

You have a tremendous range of choices in selecting the software program you will use, ranging from the elegantly simple to the enthusiastically complex. Prices for these programs vary a great deal, too, with some available as shareware (requiring only a modest payment to the authors) while others are strictly commercial (costing hundreds of dollars). You must decide, ultimately, what you want from a program and, more importantly, what you need from it.

If you're tempted to buy a high-end program that not only allows you to dial into a remote commercial database system but will also help you define your search and select the proper database services, you'll find vendors ready to sell it to you. Some of these programs are published by database vendors and publishers and some by third parties, but they have a common aim—to make the use of the online database as easy and non-threatening as possible. You might conclude that the target market for such a program includes many more lay people than information professionals, and you would be right. For that reason, you may find such a program more cumbersome than you would like.

On the other hand, there are programs that offer you the opportunity to customize the software for your individual needs. Such programs are available as commercial programs (such as Relay Silver from VM Personal Computing) and as shareware (such as Procomm). If you have an interest in working your way through the insides of a program to tweak out every bit of performance, this approach will appeal to you. Using a combination of macros and scripts (which you and the program create together), you can develop just the kind of communications program you need.

You probably fall between the two extremes of the complete software and online novice and the computer hacker (in the original, positive sense of the term). And, as you might imagine, there are software products available that are responsive to your needs. These programs do not try to do everything for you, nor do they assume that you want to do everything yourself.

One such program, that one that will serve as the example here, is DIALOGLINK, available from—that's correct—DIALOG. Not a terribly complicated communications program, it does offer some advantages to the information broker who frequently searches DIALOG. A feature that could be of particular interest to you is the Account Manager function of the program. With the Account Manager, you can keep track of your online expenses on a per search basis and print out a report of these expenses. If you treat online costs as a pass-through expense, this feature can speed your accounting and billing procedures.

You probably should avoid programs at either extreme. First, while a hand-holding program that offers everything might appeal to someone with a deeply seated fear of online searching, that particular phobia is not commonly found in successful information brokers. In fact, the professional online searcher probably would tire very quickly of the intrusion of such a program. At the other extreme, while staying up nights working to make a piece of software jump through various hoops might be an enticing preoccupation, it is not a particularly rewarding one and your time might be better spent organizing, running and marketing your service.

While DIALOGLINK does allow you to access other services, we will only look at how it works with DIALOG here. It is a lot less flexible than Procomm and less powerful than ProSearch, but for many of you, it could serve very well.

Searching with DIALOGLINK

To offer some consistency, the search premise used in the demonstration of EasyNet will once again be employed. You'll check DIALINDEX (File 411) to determine the most likely databases for further search. You'll conduct those searches, download a few sample records and there the session will end. The examination of DIALOGLINK will not, however, end there. You'll also discover the program's ability to produce a search session invoice and cover sheet.

The following files will be used for the DIALINDEX search:

Philosopher's Index	File 57
Social Scisearch	File 7
Sociological Abstracts	File 37
Religion Index	File 190

Any files searched after these will be selected based on the results of the DIALINDEX search. The Religion Index, which produced the only hits during the EasyNet search, is included to ensure some positive results of the search. The search phrase to be used is:

think(w)tank? and religio?

On the next page begins the transcript (slightly edited for space and clarity) of this rather simplistic search. Again, the transcript appears on the right and explanatory comments on the left, and the searcher's input is in **bold**.

```
Welcome to DIALOG
Dialog level 13.7.8 B
COPR. (c) DIALOG INFORMATION SERVICES, INC. ALL RIGHTS
RESERVED.
NO CLAIM TO ORIG. U.S. GOVT. WORKS.
File  1:ERIC - 66-87/AUG
    Set Items Description
    --- ----- -----------
```

DIALINDEX (File 411) is selected.

```
? b 411
    18sep87 00:44:11 User000000
    $0.12  0.004 Hrs File1
    $0.07 DialnetW
    $0.19 Estimated cost this file
    $0.19 Estimated total session cost  0.004 Hrs.


File 411:DIALINDEX(tm)
(Copr. DIALOG Inf.Ser.Inc.)
? sf 57, 7, 37, 190
```

The four files named above (and below) are selected.

```
File 57:  PHILOSOPHERS INDEX - 40-87/JUL
File  7:  SOCIAL SCISEARCH - 72-87/WK32
File 37:  SOCIOLOGICAL ABSTRACTS 63-87/ISSUE2
File 190: RELIGION INDEX - 1949-1987/APR

File    Items Description
----    ----- -----------
```

The search term is entered.

```
? s think(w)tank? and religio?

 57: PHILOSOPHERS INDEX - 40-87/JUL
```

File 57 shows no hits on the search term.

```
        703 THINK
          4 TANK?
          2 THINK(W)TANK?
      13854 RELIGIO?
          0 THINK(W)TANK? AND RELIGIO?


  7: SOCIAL SCISEARCH - 72-87/WK32
```

File 7 shows no hits on the search term.

```
        557 THINK
        199 TANK?
         38 THINK(W)TANK?
       8230 RELIGIO?
          0 THINK(W)TANK? AND RELIGIO?


 37: SOCIOLOGICAL ABSTRACTS 63-87/ISSUE2
```

File 37 shows one hit on the search term.

```
        599 THINK
         47 TANK?
         17 THINK(W)TANK?
      13771 RELIGIO?
          1 THINK(W)TANK? AND RELIGIO?
```

File 190 shows two hits on the search term (the EasyNet search gave 5 hits).

```
190: RELIGION INDEX - 1949-1987/APR
        223 THINK
         36 TANK?
          6 THINK(W)TANK?
      47885 RELIGIO?
          2 THINK(W)TANK? AND RELIGIO?
? b 37
```

File 37 is selected in order to conduct the search there.

```
    18sep87 00:44:36 User000000
$0.31  0.007 Hrs File411
$0.12 DialnetW
$0.43 Estimated cost this file
$0.62 Estimated total session cost  0.011 Hrs.


File 37:SOCIOLOGICAL ABSTRACTS 63-87/ISSUE2
(Copr. Soc. Abstracts)

   Set Items Description
   --- ----- -----------
? ss think(w)tank? and religio?
```

Again, one hit results from the search request, just like DIALINDEX said it would.

```
   S1    599 THINK
   S2     47 TANK?
   S3     17 THINK(W)TANK?
   S4  13771 RELIGIO?
   S5      1 THINK(W)TANK? AND RELIGIO?

? type 5/5/1
```

This is the record (edited for space) that resulted from this search in File 37.

```
5/5/1
2013989  86Q6267
Backward through the Looking Glass
Hoos, Ida R.
U California, Berkeley 94720
Technological Forecasting and Social Change 1985, 28, 4,
Dec, 287-295.
CODEN:TFSCB3
Pub. Year: 1985
Country of Publication: United States
Language: English
Document Type: Abstract of Journal Article (aja)
Availability: Hardcopy reproduction available from UMI, Ann
    Arbor MI
Taking a retrospective glance at the progress & power of
technology in its various manifestations during the past
half century, how the ....
                       .....
```

References. AA
Descriptors: Technological Progress (D857100); Technology (D857400)
Identifiers: technology, manifestations/effects;
Section Headings: policy, planning, forecasting- planning & forecasting
(2454)
? **b 190**

> 18sep87 00:45:32 User000000
> $0.96 0.016 Hrs File37
> $0.20 1 Types in Format 5
> $0.20 1 Types
> $0.28 DialnetW
> $1.44 Estimated cost this file
> $2.06 Estimated total session cost 0.026 Hrs.

File 190:RELIGION INDEX - 1949-1987/APR
Copr. Amer. Theological Library Assoc.

> Set Items Description
> --- ----- -----------
? **ss think(w)tank? and religio?**

> S1   223 THINK
> S2   36 TANK?
> S3   6 THINK(W)TANK?
> S4 47885 RELIGIO?
> S5   2 THINK(W)TANK? AND RELIGIO?
? **type 5/5/1-2**

5/5/1
0061811 002478
FUTURISM: ITS IMPLICATIONS FOR RELIGIOUS EDUCATION
THOMPSON, NORMA H
ST LUKE J, 18, 150-174, MR 1975
Language: English
RELIGIOUS EDUCATORS SHOULD TAKE SERIOUSLY STUDIES OF THE FUTURE FOR THE INSIGHTS AND UNDERSTANDINGS THEY PROVIDE FOR DECISION MAKING IN
        .....
Descriptors: FUTUROLOGY; RELIGIOUS EDUCATION

5/5/2
0003316 253756
THE DESTRUCTION OF CITIES AND THE RITUAL OF WAR
MANCHESTER, PETER B
BOOK FORUM, 6 NO 3, 286-292, 1983
Language: English
THE STUDY OF RELIGIOUS MYTH AND RITUAL THROWS LIGHT ON THE CONNECTION BETWEEN RELIGION AND WAR IN A DIFFERENT DIMENSION THAN

File 190 (Religion Index) is chosen in order to conduct the search there.

These are the two records (edited for space) that resulted from this search in File 190.

```
                                    •••••
                        Descriptors: WAR--RELIGIOUS ASPECTS; RITUAL;
                        ASSYRO-BABYLONIAN RELIGION; STATE AND RELIGION; KINGS AND
                        RULERS (IN RELIGION, FOLKLORE); ATOMIC WEAPONS
                        ? logoff
```

The search is complete
and the logoff command is
given.

```
                           18sep87 00:46:03 User000000
                        $0.43  0.009 Hrs File190
                        $0.00 2 Types in Format 5
                        $0.00 2 Types
                        $0.16 DialnetW
                        $0.59 Estimated cost this file
                        $2.65 Estimated total session cost  0.035 Hrs.
```

This, obviously, is not meant to be an exhaustive examination of how to conduct a proper search on DIALOG. This is only the most rudimentary search, conducted only to demonstrate the workings of DIALOGLINK. Reproduced in Fig. 6-1 is the DIALOG Search Session Invoice produced following this search.

This invoice allows you to perform some very useful functions. For example, you can assign several variables to the search, including:

Subject	Client Name
Charge Code	Searcher
Job Number	

These can all be used by you to keep track of your work for each client. In addition, the report gives you a file-by-file report on the search and the costs incurred. Take a look at the report from one file.

Time of search = > 00:44

File searched = > DIALOG FILE 37

Summary of the = >	Connect	$0.96
different = >	Types	0.20
charges = >	Prints	0.00
incurred in = >	Print Credits	0.00
this file. = >	Reports	0.00
= >	Communications	0.28

Total charges &
connect time. = > Total: $1.44 Connect Hours: 0.016

Other summaries (by date, file, searcher, client, etc.) are available, and many of them would be useful to you if, as previously suggested, you are doing a lot of searching on DIALOG.

```
===========================================================================
                      DIALOG SEARCH SESSION INVOICE
===========================================================================
   Subject:        Think Tanks and Religion
   Client Name:    I. Emma Client
   Charge Code:    Retainer (10%)
   Searcher:       John H. Everett
   Date:           September 18, 1987
   Job No.:        00001
---------------------------------------------------------------------------
   00:43
   DIALOG FILE 1
     Connect       $  0.12
     Types            0.00
     Prints           0.00
     Print Credits    0.00
     Reports          0.00
     Communications   0.07
     Total:        $  0.19   Connect Hours: 0.004
   00:44
   DIALOG FILE 411
     Connect       $  0.31
     Types            0.00
     Prints           0.00
     Print Credits    0.00
     Reports          0.00
     Communications   0.12
     Total:        $  0.43   Connect Hours: 0.007
   00:44
   DIALOG FILE 37
     Connect       $  0.96
     Types            0.20
     Prints           0.00
     Print Credits    0.00
     Reports          0.00
     Communications   0.28
     Total:        $  1.44   Connect Hours: 0.016
   00:45
   DIALOG FILE 190
     Connect       $  0.43
     Types            0.00
     Prints           0.00
     Print Credits    0.00
     Reports          0.00
     Communications   0.16
     Total:        $  0.59   Connect Hours: 0.009
---------------------------------------------------------------------------
               September 17, 1987  10:50pm  Page 1
   Total Session Cost: $  2.65
   Total Connect Hours:   0.036
```

Fig. 6-1. Typical invoice from a DIALOG search session, produced with the DIALOGLINK Account Manager.

Full-Text Databases

As the online information business continues to evolve, the directions it takes are often determined by what the people who use the system want; that is what is meant by "market driven." It is also true that the directions are often determined by what the database producers and vendors think you want. But it's not always the people who use the system whose wants are taken into consideration. Quite often, the vendors and producers will make decisions based on what they think people who *don't* use the system might want—even if that's not what you want. In that way, they hope to attract new people to the service.

When online information was the exclusive province of the information professional, the available databases were predominantly *reference databases*. In other words, the information in the databases was not the information actually being sought, but directions to that information. Therefore, if someone wanted a collection of articles on a given subject, an online search was conducted to identify those articles, but the articles themselves had to be obtained through more conventional methods.

A subset of the information industry was created to answer the need created by the reference databases: document delivery. Today, some of the major information services are making substantial incomes through document delivery. As the number of full-text databases increases in proportion to the number of reference databases, this need for document delivery will decrease.

Why have full-text databases emerged? As has already been pointed out, the online industry is in the midst of a major effort to interest what it calls the end-user market. If successful, this effort will bring the people who need and utilize information to the keyboards to find it for themselves.

Database vendors are using a number of methods to attract this end-user market. DIALOG Information Services' Business Connection program is a direct move to attract more business information users to the keyboard. Front-end software programs that add a "user-friendly" interface to online access also are aimed at the end market. And gateway services such as EasyNet, that bring together a number of different database services under one roof, are yet another such effort.

So, too, are *full-text databases*. By giving the searcher not just a reference, but the actual text of the material, the database service eliminates a step (document location and delivery) that will nearly always involve the use of an information professional. This is not, by the way, some kind of nasty conspiracy on the part of the online community to make the information professional obsolete. It is, rather, their attempt to increase their market size and share.

These full-text databases are also sauce for the gander, and you can use them to your advantage. On the most basic level, you can eliminate one step in your research process because now you won't have to contact a document delivery service in order to provide your client with full-text information. This saves time and money and improves your response time and profit margin.

Full-text databases also eliminate the abstracter from the process. Instead of relying on a third party's summary of what was said in an article, you can now search exactly what was said in the article. While abstracters have done a superlative job for many years, many people welcome the chance to search the complete text of a document because they feel it gives them a finer sense of control and helps them pinpoint the documents they need.

Often, however, the use of full-text databases can have the opposite effect. Because of the size of each record, there are simply more chances for a false response to occur. As a result, you can capture many more records that are not related to your topic. To an extent, this drawback is countered by the continued availability of *field searching*. This allows you to continue to use the more limited, and thus more focused, vocabulary of a bibliographic database either alone or in concert with full-text searching. Used properly, this can, indeed, result in more accurate searching.

Full-text databases alone will not attract the end-user to the world of online information, but they are a significant development in the process of making that world more immediately and clearly useful. As more full-text databases become available (and they most surely will) and as search techniques for these databases become more refined (as they, too, will), the value of the full-text database to the information professional and to the end-user will become more apparent. And this will ultimately lead to increased profits for the database vendors.

Many systems are adding to their collection of full-text databases and some systems are virtually all full-text. Included in the latter is NewsNet, a database service containing the full text of more than 300 newsletters (among other things), and VU/TEXT, a database that covers national and regional newspapers (again, among other things). Many databases available from Mead Data Central, are full-text. Older services with a great many reference databases already online are now adding full-text databases to their service. DIALOG Information Services and BRS Search Services are among them.

You can probably expect more historical databases as a result of the increase in full-text information online. Not only are current publications available because of the widespread use of electronic typesetting procedures, but older, previously published material is available both through optical scanning technology and the use of low-cost data entry operations in other countries. The most prominent example of a historical document available online may be the King James Bible, now available on DIALOG. It may not be long before you can search Plato, Shakespeare and Henry David Thoreau online. Of course, the question might be, "Is it really worth $60 per hour to search *The Republic?*"

What Else Can You Expect?

While those areas of technological advancement may represent the primary focus of the information industry at present, there are many other areas that will also affect how you work as an information broker. Some of these issues promise less of an impact on the industry, or are too far in the future for now. But it couldn't hurt to take a quick look at them.

In fact, quick is just exactly what one of these technological advancements is called—//QUICK, to be precise. Available on Dow Jones News/Retrieval, this service will search six different databases for a company name or stock symbol, so you don't have to enter and search each one of them separately. In addition, //QUICK will give you the full report on the company for a flat fee. It seems apparent that this service is aimed at the business information user who would not perform a search of all six databases independently. Also, by performing the service for a flat fee, //QUICK eliminates the fear many people have of what they perceive as high and uncontrollable online costs.

The //QUICK service asks you to specify a company by name or stock symbol and then presents you with the following menu:

PRESS FOR

1 CURRENT QUOTES
2 LATEST NEWS ON (company)
3 FINANCIAL AND MARKET OVERVIEW
4 EARNINGS ESTIMATES
5 COMPANY VS INDUSTRY PERFORMANCE
6 INCOME STATEMENTS, BAL SHEETS
7 COMPANY PROFILE
8 INSIDER TRADING SUMMARY
9 INVESTMENT RESEARCH REPORTS

TYPE ALL FOR ENTIRE COMPANY REPORT FOR $39 FLAT FEE.

TYPE PRINT FOLLOWED BY ITEM NUMBERS, SEPARATED BY COMMAS, TO PRINT SELECTED SECTIONS OF THE REPORT AT REGULAR USAGE RATES.
EXAMPLE: PRINT 1,3,9

PRESS RETURN FOR INSTRUCTIONS AND PRICING INFORMATION.

When DIALOG introduced DIALINDEX, which allows you to search any combination of databases to determine which ones are best suited to your information need, it took a step in this direction. However, DIALINDEX does not allow you to actually see the records resulting from your search, only an accounting of the number of records within each specified database. To retrieve the actual records, you must still individually search each of the databases. And, because of lingering differences in the fields, thesauruses and format of the databases, it is not possible to conduct truly comprehensive and complex searches in DIALINDEX. But in October 1987, DIALOG introduced a service called OneSearch, which does allow you to search more than one DIALOG database at a time. It will be interesting to see how this service develops and is used.

The people who actually use the information you find are not interested in looking for the information so much as they are in having it, analyzing it, and using it. For these people to do their own online searching, the search process will have to be both simple and comprehensive. In other words, the information must be available using intuitive,

English-language commands and from as few sources as possible. This is what //QUICK is designed to do.

But once again, a service designed for the end-user can be of value to the information broker. It would allow you, for example, to offer a full report on any publicly traded company for a flat fee. Your costs would be contained by the //QUICK service and you could thus offer flat-fee searches without putting yourself at risk. While this kind of service alone might not sustain an information broker, it does present an interesting marketing opportunity and a way to introduce your service to the prospective client.

Another way in which online information has become more useful is by allowing you to customize the way you receive the information. It is possible to "tag" those fields you want included in your printed or typed report and sort the records before they are printed or typed. One very obvious use is to create mailing or telemarketing lists. On DIALOG, for instance, you can ask for mailing labels to be printed (on adhesive-backed labels) from over 20 databases, including the Dun & Bradstreet databases. You can choose a special REPORT command which, when used with a SORT command, prints out a listing of, say, businesses in order of market share. And, if none of the standard report formats fit your needs, you can now customize your own report format in nearly every database on the system.

Since a lot of the time and effort you will spend as an information broker will be spent editing and manipulating the results of your search, such features will translate directly into time (and money) savings for you. Of course, these same customized reporting options will be available to every subscriber to DIALOG, including the end-user, just as //QUICK is available to every Dow Jones News/Retrieval subscriber. So you'll have to do more than simply pass through the benefits of these features to your clients. It will be nice, to be sure, to spend less time reformatting and more time analyzing or otherwise adding real value to the information.

There will continue to be advances in technology in the information industry and, one day, those tools that amaze you today will seem primitive. It is impossible to anticipate every new technology, but you should keep a watch on the area so that you can be prepared to respond to, use, and market those advances when they become available.

Chapter 7

A Sample Search

O NCE YOU'VE GOT THE BUSINESS, WHAT DO YOU DO WITH IT? THE ANSWER TO THIS QUES-
tion will depend greatly on the information needs and budget constraints of the client, but you will, sooner or later, do a search of some printed or online database to
answer a specific informational need for your client.

This chapter features a very basic sample search for a client who is thinking about
becoming an information broker. While there is no such thing as "an average search
request," you'll learn the major parts of the search process. There will be an interview
with the client wherein you discover just what he wants to know and why he wants to
know it. Then you'll develop a search strategy for the client (keeping within budget
constraints) and perform an online search. Finally, you'll review the results of the search,
package the information and deliver it to the client.

While there is no need for an actual transcript of the sample search, Chapter 9 will
contain the references resulting from this search. The search described in this chapter
was first conducted (for the first edition of this book) before the introduction of DIALOG2,
but the general principles involved remain the same. The results of the search have been
updated with current information.

The Interview Process

The interview process ought to serve a number of purposes, both for you and for
the client. For you, it is a time to explain your service—what it can and cannot do, what
it costs and why (if necessary). You also can submit your contract/letter of agreement

for consideration or signature and collect any prepayment, if appropriate. For the client, it is a time to clearly delineate the information need he has and why he has it, what his budgetary and time constraints might be, etc. It is also a time for the client to seek reinforcement for his decision to use your services.

Some clients may consider it an admission of failure to use outside assistance, whether that assistance is from an information broker, a temporary clerk or a technical consultant. In addition, some clients may consider your services too expensive, regardless of your fees, their relationship to fees charged by other information brokers, and the costs of doing the research another way or of doing without it altogether. You must be able to determine which of these reservations your client may have (and he may have more than one) and be able to deal with them before they become an obstacle to getting the assignment.

A book like this cannot teach you how to read people effectively, though other books try. To successfully sell yourself and your business, you will need this skill, so plan to devote some time to it. In response to the reservations suggested above, you could point out that seeking outside help is not an admission of failure, it is a sign of good management—making the most of available resources. Setting fees in response to your costs of operation and as a marketing decision was discussed in Chapter 4. If you have followed those guidelines, then you should have no difficulty in discussing your fees with the client. However, you should be prepared to show the client how much other methods of research can cost and how much not having the information can cost.

The Scenario

For the purposes of this chapter, your client is a middle manager in a large snack food corporation. This middle manager has been in charge of the engineering services department, which includes maintenance of a small library of printed material of interest to the engineers. They use a computer-assisted design system in this company, so the manager is somewhat familiar with computers through work. In addition, he bought a home computer so the kids can play video games.

This manager has seen some mention in one of the corporate library-related magazines about information brokering and thinks he might be able to go into that line of work. He has saved up a little money and really wants out of a company job which shows little promise of true advancement. However, he knows that he must do a great deal of studying about information brokering before he quits his job and hangs out his shingle.

Since he subscribes to these corporate library-related publications in your area, he received a brochure from you as a part of your direct marketing campaign (you rented the mailing list). After considering how much time it would take to personally visit the library and try to find some more information about information brokering, he decides to call you and ask for help. (The obvious question about conflict of interest—helping someone who might well turn out to be your competitor—will be ignored here. After all, this is just hypothetical.)

The Reference Interview

Chris Dobson, manager of the library at INFOMART, has conducted a great many reference interviews in the course of her career. When asked to suggest the course of such an interview with this client, she offered the following:

Client: What do you have on information brokering?

Broker: What kind of information did you need?

Client: Oh, just whatever you have.

Broker: Do you need to know

- Who is doing it, or
- How to set up a brokerage, or
- What the market is like for brokers, or
- What brokers usually charge, or
- What databases are available for searching?

Client: I think I'd like recent articles on how businesses are using information brokers, what services brokers offer, and how they market them.

The search that follows would be in response to that request (essentially, the third item from the above list). While this is a simplified version of the reference interview, it does offer a valuable glimpse into the client/broker relationship. You'll notice that the client begins with only a vague understanding of what he needs and is led to a more specific request by the broker. When presented with a list of options, the client was perfectly capable of deciding what he wanted.

Dobson further suggested that, had the client chosen different questions, the responses would be as follows:

- Who is doing it—a directory of brokers, such as *The Directory of Fee-Based Information Services* from Burwell Enterprises.

- How to set up a brokerage—this book.

- What brokers usually charge—again, Burwell's directory.

- What databases are available—a directory of databases, such as the one available from Cuadra/Elsevier.

The Needs

During the course of the interview, you determine the following things about this client:

He is interested in a form of "Instant Education" about information brokering.

He wants reading material—books, magazine and newspaper articles, etc.

He would like to know about any professional organizations that he could join.

He would like to find out what kinds of ads information brokers run.

He really doesn't want to spend too much money.

He is not in a rush for the information.

Your Evaluation

Based on these considerations, you make the following determinations:

You should use only one database vendor, if possible, to help keep costs under control.

You should have the vendor print out most of the records if this helps reduce the cost.

You should look at the general press, the business press and indexes of advertising.

The client approves your estimate of the search costs, makes a small prepayment and will look for delivery of the results of the search within a week to ten days.

Search Strategy

Based on your interview with the client, you know you are going to have to keep your online time to a minimum. The way you do this, of course, is to carefully think through your search options and your search strategy before you sign on to any database. Earlier you noted that you probably would need to confine your search to a single database vendor in order to try to keep the search costs to a minimum. Therefore, you are going to need a vendor that offers a large number of databases covering the areas you need: the general press, the business press and advertising indices. For this search, DIALOG Information Services will be used; you may have or develop other preferences that would lead you to another service. While the actual search techniques will vary from service to service, the offline work should not.

You can begin your planning of this search request in several areas: picking the databases to search, determining the search terms to use, etc. The search begins by fully defining and limiting the search terms.

Selecting the Terms

Obviously, one of the search terms you need to use is "information broker." However, this is a fairly new term and many people do not think it accurately describes what a broker does. These people tend to use terms such as "information gathering service" or "fee-based information service" or "information retrieval service."

In DIALOG, as in most online database service, the system operates on the principles of *Boolean logic* (what you may remember as set logic from math). Boolean logic uses three operators to describe the relationship between, in this case, terms: "AND", "OR" and "NOT". In Boolean logic, if you specify "A OR B" then you are asking for every occurrence of either A or B in a record in the database. If you specify "A AND B" then you are asking for every occurrence of both A and B in a record. If you specify "A NOT B" then you are asking for every record that contains A but does not contain B.

In this example, then, you are looking for "information broker" OR "information gathering service" OR "fee-based information service" OR "information retrieval service." DIALOG allows you to use certain techniques to simplify your search. One is *truncation*, which permits you to allow for different forms of the same word. For example, to allow for "gather," "gathers," "gathered" or "gathering" in the example above, you could use "gather?" instead of each of the four. Due to the way the system operates, using a literal space in a search phrase, such as "information broker" tends to restrict the response. DIALOG allows you to use an operator that indicates a certain order and proximity of terms—"(W)." So instead of using "information broker," you would use "information(W)broker."

Each specific database has certain search aids, such as restricted vocabularies, descriptors and the ability to limit searches in a variety of ways. You will be doing full-text searches, i.e., searching for any occurrence of any of the terms anywhere in the record. Full-text searching will be adequate for this search, but not for every search. The vendors will offer you training more advanced than this, and the database providers can offer search aids for their database. In general, you should take advantage of these resources if you plan to use a specific database with any frequency.

Given your needs, then, you would define your search terms as follows, for the purpose of full-text searching across several databases on DIALOG:

INFORMATION(W)BROKER? OR INFORMATION(W)GATHER?(W)SERVICE?
OR FEE(W)BASED(W)INFORMATION(W)SERVICE? OR INFORMATION(W)
RETRIEVAL(W)SERVICE?

Notice that the "(W)" operator was used instead of the hyphen in "fee-based." Truncation was used for broker (brokers), gather (gathers and gathering) and service (services). This is all very straightforward and more combinations of these terms (and others) could be used to refine the search. To illustrate the search process, however, these terms will suffice.

Now that the search terms have been selected, it is time to select the databases.

Selecting the Databases

One of the characteristics of DIALOG that some might call a shortcoming is the fact that you can search only one database at a time. Thus, if you would like to look for information in a series of databases, you must do it sequentially. DIALOG does a couple of things, however, to compensate for this. DIALOG gives you the ability to save the search terms used in one database and use them in another by simply asking the system to execute the saved search terms. This can be a timesaver when you use lengthy terms consistently in a number of databases.

In addition, DIALOG offers a database called DIALINDEX™. This database allows you to sample a large number of different databases to see how many ''hits'' you get from your search request from each. While you cannot actually search these databases from DIALINDEX, it will allow you to avoid searching those databases with few or no hits and to identify those that have a large number of hits. It will also allow you to identify possible problems in your search terms that might result in far too many or too few hits.

One of the features of DIALINDEX is the ability to call up a number of databases using DIALOG-assigned names for groups of databases likely to be of common interest to a searcher. The two used in this search are BUSNEWS and BUSTEXT, for business news and business text. In addition, certain specific databases not included in one of the two groups named above but of use in this search will be selected. The databases used for the DIALINDEX search are:

ABI/INFORM (© Data Courier, Inc.)
ADTRACK (© Corporate Intelligence, Inc.)
Magazine Index (© Information Access Corp.)
PAIS International (© Public Affairs Information Service, Inc.)
Management Contents (© Management Contents)
Economic Abstracts International (offered by Learned Information)
National Newspaper Index (© Information Access Corp.)
Encyclopedia of Associations (© compiled by Gale Research Co.)
Standard & Poor's Daily News (© Standard & Poor's Corp.)
Economic Literature Index (© American Economic Association)
Trade and Industry Index (© Information Access Corp.)
Health Planning and Administration (produced by the U.S. National Library of Medicine)
Insurance Abstracts (© Xerox Corp.)
Harfax Industry Data Sources (© Harper & Row, Publishers, Inc.)
NEWSEARCH (© Information Access Corp.)
Books in Print (© R. R. Bowker Co.)

Using DIALINDEX

You can sign on to DIALOG, select DIALINDEX, select the files above, run the search and sign off for well under $10. Once offline, you can review the number of hits for each individual search term and the total search request (using the OR operator) for each individual database and determine which ones warrant a search. Since you asked DIALOG to save the search logic you used before you signed off the system, you only have to ask for that logic to be run when you sign on to the databases, saving typing time and costs. DIALOG will save this logic for the rest of the day at no charge. You also can alter your search request if the number of "hits" are so high or so low as to require it.

A transcript of the search of DIALINDEX will not be reproduced here (you did see one in Chapter 6), but some of the responses that were received will be discussed as well as what those responses might indicate. One of the nice features of DIALOG is its ability to show you the number of hits for each search term in your search request in addition to the total number of hits for your search request. Thus you know how many instances of "information broker" were found, how many instances of "information gathering service," etc., in addition to how many of any one of the terms used (remember the OR operator). For instance, in ABI/INFORM, you had fourteen hits on "IN-FORMATION(W)BROKER?" and fourteen on "INFORMATION(W)RETRIEVAL (W)SERVICE?" and none on the others for a total of 28 hits. This tells you that the records containing "information broker" are completely different from those containing "Information Retrieval Service." Since the latter may refer to a form of internal information management, you ought to be cautious about it.

Another interesting development in this search was the response from the Health Planning and Administration database. This database indicated three hits for "INFOR-MATION(W)BROKER?" and four for "INFORMATION(W)RETRIEVAL(W)SER-VICE?" for a total of seven records. By contrast, Insurance Abstracts, gave zero hits all across the board. This may be an indication of one profession that already recognizes the role of the information broker more than others.

The Final Search

Based on the results of your use of DIALINDEX, you decide to return to DIALOG and search the following databases: ABI/INFORM, with 28 hits; ADTRACK, with 158 hits; Magazine Index, with 33 hits; PAIS International, with 15 hits; Management Contents, with 11 hits; National Newspaper Index, with 2 hits; Encyclopedia of Associations, with 1 hit; Standard & Poor's Daily News, with 4 hits; Trade and Industry Index, with 21 hits; Harfax Industry Data Sources, with 9 hits; NEWSEARCH, with 2 hits; and Books in Print, with 6 hits.

This is where speed is of prime importance, for there are many databases to search and many records to select. Fortunately, you can use the search logic you saved from the earlier search; that will save you some time. In addition, you will ask DIALOG to print out the majority of the records, though you should always review at least a few of the hits to make sure you are getting what you want. If a database has only 3 or 4 hits, you can display those and print them out in your office. But for many more, it becomes more economical to have DIALOG print them out and mail them to you. All of this assumes, of course, that you have contacted DIALOG and the above named database providers and secured their permission to act as a broker for third party use of their databases.

The Package and Delivery

You will receive the printout of your search results from DIALOG within a few days. DIALOG provides you with a very nicely packaged report. The records are printed in landscape format (that is, sideways) on 8.5" × 11" cut paper. The print quality is excellent, which is good because it is also very small. The title of the article or record is emphasized, making it easy to distinguish during reading. Each database gets a separate package, even though you searched them at the same time using the same search request. Each package has a cover sheet specifying the database searched and giving you a place for your client's name and address and for yours.

With the permission of DIALOG and the database providers, you can simply attach a cover letter, add the appropriate names and addresses to the report(s), highlight any items of specific interest, and send the report on to your client. For an example of the kinds of references obtained during the actual search of these databases, see Chapter 9.

General Search Tips

Each search you perform will be different. In this search, you have barely touched on many of the characteristics of computer databases, search techniques, printed resources, etc. However, this chapter should provide you with a superficial look at a simple search. This will not act as a substitute for the training seminars offered by the various database vendors nor for your experience and training. Here are a few tips that you may not get in the formal training programs.

You will learn that there is always more to learn about online searching and, indeed, research in general. And often it is easy to forget even the most basic techniques in the heat of the search. For instance, an experienced online searcher, who should have known better, tells of an experience he had while searching an electronics database. One of his search terms was "ceramic?" and this term turned out to be a part of nearly every record in the database. When the system "went away" for a long time, he realized his error, but, by then, it was too late. He could only wait until the system returned to inform him that there were hundreds of thousands of records in the database that contained the word "ceramic." By then, he had figured that out. This is the same mistake that was made in the search of Religion Index on EasyNet (see Chapter 6).

Another example of the importance of synonyms in your search strategy: "At one time I did a MEDLINE search," says Chris Wessellman, "and I was looking for something on adolescents or pediatric cases. I didn't find many hits. It had not occurred to me to use the synonym 'youth.' But 'youth' is very important in MEDLINE. You have to be thinking about things like that."

In a presentation entitled, "How to Avoid Common Search Miztakes," (sic) DIA-LOG provides a checklist of some common mistakes, including:

- Inappropriate database.
- Too many concepts.
- "AND" used when "OR" was meant.
- Truncation needed.
- Typing or spelling error.
- Incorrect set number used in search statement.
- Did not space around words or connectors.
- Parentheses not used or used incorrectly.

The training you will take from the online database vendors and producers (and you *will* take this training) will help you learn how to search the database and services they offer. These training sessions do very little to teach you about general search techniques, however. For example, you can refine your search in a number of ways in order to get just the right number of records. Too often a search will result in either too many or too few records. If you get too many records, you don't have a truly useful body of information. You'll still have to read through all those records to find the ones that you need. If, on the other hand, you get too few records, you may not have fully covered the subject matter that interests you. While there is no formula to determine the "right" number of records, you can use certain techniques to make your search as comprehensive as possible without making it too broad.

Pearl Growing and Fractions

There are a great many formal search techniques, each known by more than one name. Two techniques will be discussed here—one is designed to start with a very small number of records and add to it, while the other is designed to start with a large number of records and weed out the irrelevant ones. These two techniques are called (among other things), *pearl growing* and *fractions*, respectively.

Pearl growing works just as the image suggests. You begin with a very restrictive search request that will produce a very small number of records. You then review those records (or, in some cases, that record) to see what index terms are used. Based on the results of this study, you broaden your search request and repeat the process until your search turns up no new index terms that are relevant to your interest. At that point, you have completed your search.

Fractions works in just the opposite way. A very general search request is used to capture a very large number of records. If that number of records is too large to be manageable (as is most likely will be), you add a second search request to the first, resulting in a smaller number of records. As with pearl growing, you should review a few of the records retrieved in the first search to find index terms that you can use in the subsequent steps. When the number of records retrieved is small enough, you have completed the search. With this technique, you must be careful about the order in which you add the more restrictive search requests. If you restrict the search request too quickly, you may overcorrect and retrieve too few records.

Database Service Selection

If the information you need can only be found in one database, and that database can only be found on one service, you have no selection problem. All you have to do is find that database and gain access to it. Often, however, the information you need will be available from more than one source. In those instances, you will have to compare the sources and determine which one is best for your purposes. This will include times when an online source for the information is not the best option.

When faced with the task of choosing the best online source for your information, you will have two choices to make: the database you will use and the service you will use. These choices are separate and distinct from one another and they will be examined in turn.

To choose the best database, you should examine each one, asking the following questions:

What purpose does the database attempt to serve? While it is sometimes possible to use a database in a different way than it was intended to be used, most often your intended use must match the purpose of the database. For instance, if you need full-text articles from the professional legal press, it would not do to search a database that contains bibliographic citations for popular consumer magazines.

What are the sources used in creating the database? All databases that claim to cover business periodicals do not include the same periodicals for the same period of time. One database might offer abstracts from 250 different business publications. Another might offer just the citations from 2,000 different publications. A third might offer the full text of the articles from 50 different publications.

You should ask questions, not only of the database, but of the vendor, as well. These would include:

What search tools are available to you? Does the database or service offer you the search aids you need to be able to find the information you need? Is the search language powerful enough? What fields can be searched? Is the thesaurus extensive and current enough? If the information you need is in the database, but you can't get at it, it doesn't do you any good.

How current is the database? This is not just a question of how frequently the database is uploaded, though that is one consideration. Also important is the age of the information being added to the database. For example, if the database is updated quarterly, but the information included in each update is two to five months old, you won't find the most recent information.

How far back does the database go? If you're looking for information from a specific point in time, you must make sure the database covers that point in time. For instance, if you wanted to search the Dallas Morning News on DataTimes for information on the Republican National Convention in the summer of 1984, you would be disappointed to learn that coverage of The Dallas Morning News did not begin until November of 1984.

You should direct questions about the age and currency of a database to the producer of the database. Someone there can alert you to the differences in each vendor's version of that database—differences in coverage, update frequency, update currency, etc.

In selecting the best online vendor for the database, you should ask the following questions:

Is the database service accessible to you? Is it available through one of the packet switching networks that serve your area? If not, does it have an (800) number you can call to access the service? If you need to make extensive use of a database service that is only available via long distance, you may find the cost prohibitive.

Is the database service available when you need it? If you're going to do a lot of your searching late at night or on the weekends, is the service available during those times? If there's no one home when you call, you can't use the service.

How much does the database cost? No two database vendors charge you in exactly the same way. In addition to the hourly (or per minute) cost, there are a host of additional costs for everything from taking up the CPU's time to having records displayed on your screen to having records printed out and mailed to you to how many records satisfy your search request.

While you've got to keep watch on your costs, there comes a point where making distinctions between pennies is not worth the effort. If you're going to pass through the search costs to your client, you'll have a responsibility to that client to keep online costs within reason. But if you're charging for your time while planning the search, how much can you save your client compared to how much you'll charge her for saving a bit of online cost?

More than cost, what you should consider primarily in selecting a database are the other factors outlined above. If you pick a database that includes the information you need and gives you the tools you need to get that information, you'll be doing a good job for your client in keeping online costs to a minimum.

Search Request Forms

At some point in your development of your search strategy, you'll use a form of some kind to help you devise your strategy and request. No one form is right and, in fact, some database services supply you with sample search request forms designed for use with their databases. What you will need will depend on your situation, but here are some general guidelines.

First, you must determine whether you or your client will be filling out the form or whether you'll both be working on it. How you design your form will depend on your plans for it.

If you'll be using the form, you should design it to work throughout the search process, from the interview through the filing of the finished report. The form should guide you through the interview process, giving you plenty of room to record your client's answers. It should include a worksheet so you can develop your search strategy and record your final search request. You should also have a space to record the results of that search strategy and to refine it further, if necessary. Finally, you should have a spot to record the results of the search (along with such basic information as date, time, cost, etc.). You can even use the form to track billing and collection and as a permanent record of the transaction. Of course, it would have to be a pretty wonderful (and sturdy) form to do all that, but you get the general idea.

If your client will be using the form, it will have to be much more basic and self-explanatory. Your client will have to be able to understand your questions (without you being there to help) and be guided to giving you answers that will be useful to you. First-time or infrequent clients and those with more complex search needs will probably not be able to use this type of form. You can, however, get them to fill in their name and address and give you a general idea of their information need. You can also ask them to sign it after you've written in an estimate or price cap as an agreement to pay for the costs of the search.

If you and your client both will be using the form, just be sure you make it clear which sections are your responsibility and which sections are the client's. You don't want the client worrying over your areas and you wouldn't want to scare a client away with an intimidating form.

Figure 7-1 is the search request form used by the Multnomah County Library in Portland, Ore., as a part of their online search service. Figure 7-2 is a form developed by Chris Wesselman for his own use (though he credits the forms used by several other brokers). Figure 7-3 is a sample search planning form which should give you an idea of another approach to developing your own forms. Don't dwell too long on this part, but do try to develop a workable system before you start.

Now it's time to meet two information brokers who have taken very different paths into this line of work and who take two different approaches to making it work for them.

IN DEPTH SEARCH REQUEST
MULTNOMAH COUNTY LIBRARY

Date _____   Log No. _____

Name _____   Address _____

Telephone _____   _____

Library Card _____   _____

1. Description of topic (please be specific and use complete sentences).

   _____

   _____

   _____

2. List <u>synonyms</u>, key words, and technical or scientific terms not mentioned
   in your description.

   TERM   SYNONYM

   _____   _____

   _____   _____

   _____   _____

   _____   _____

3. Write a perfect imaginary article title. _____

   _____

4. Indexes and abstracts consulted:

   Title _____   Subject Heading _____

   Title _____   Subject Heading _____

5. Important authors: _____

   _____

Fig. 7-1. Multnomah County Library search request form.

6. Do you want the search limited by date? YES _____ NO _____

   If yes, what years? _____ to _____

7. Are there any aspects of the subject in which you are <u>not</u> interested?

   _____

8. Indicate scope of material wanted (check one):

   ___ comprehensive search; all relevant citations, including some peripheral
       material

   ___ narrow search; only very relevant citations, possibly missing some

   ___ an approach somewhere in between

9. Indicate level of material wanted (check one):

   ___ general/non-technical OR ___ in-depth/technical

10. Types of publications desired: ___all ___journal articles ___books

    ___technical reports ___conference papers ___English language only

    ___other language (specify) _____

11. What type of results do you want?

    ___ 1. citation only

    ___ 2. citation and abstract (more expensive)

12. I agree to pay the Library Association of Portland for a computerized
    bibliographic search. Costs include: $5.00 fee, Telecommunications and
    On-line search time, printing costs plus 10% surcharge. I understand LAP
    does not guarantee that all citations will be relevant. I understand that
    no charges can be refunded once the search is completed. (The cost of
    searches vary depending on the topic and the database searched. Actual
    costs cannot be calculated until the search is completed.)

Signed _____

Indicate the maximum amount you wish to spend _____

(Fig. 7-1 continues.)

SUMMARY SHEET

1. Search conducted by: _____

2. Off-line preparation time: _____

3. Databases searched (Please place an asterisk next to any database which did

   not provide citations.): _____

   _____

   _____

   _____

4. Total cost of search: $_____

5. Search strategy: _____

   _____

   _____

(Fig. 7-1 ends.)

Date in: _____   Date due: _____   Date out: _____

NAME: _____   COMPANY: _____

Address: _____

Telephone: _____   Elec. Mail: _____

SEARCH REQUEST: What is the purpose of this project?
_____

_____

Please describe in your own words – as specifically as possible – the subject
of your search request. Be sure to indicate synonymous or alternative
terminology. If you are looking for information on a company, product, or
concept, and you already know of one that "fits" your search parameters, **please
tell us.** This can short-cut our strategy significantly and save you a lot of
money. Please also tell us that information that you definitely don't want,
i. e., oil not natural gas. Caution: this means oil only and could remove
information containing oil and gas together.

_____

_____

_____

SEARCH LIMITATIONS:

Geographic	**Type of Information**	**Statistics**	**Material**
__ USA only	__ Market Data	__ All	__ Articles
__ Worldwide	__ Products & Processes	__ Historical	__ Reports
__ Countries:	__ Company Information	__ Forecasts	__ Conferences
	__ Regulations	__ All	__ Newsletters
_____		__ Years:	__ Statistics
_____		_____	__ Other _____

YEARS OF COVERAGE	**LANGUAGE**	**FORMAT**	**OTHER LIMITS**
	__ English Only	__ Raw Data	
_____	__ Other _____	__ Edited	_____
		__ Finished Report	

BUDGET	**EXPECTED NUMBER OF ARTICLES, REPORTS, ETC.**	**Current Awareness/SDI**
	__ Small number (1 – 10)	Do you need updates
_____	__ Moderate number (11 – 30)	__ Weekly
	__ Large number (31+)	__ Monthly

Please use reverse side for additional information

Fig. 7-2. Search request form from Chris Wesselman, Research One.

SEARCHER: _____   CLIENT: _____   DATE: _____   DUE: _____

QUESTION: _____
_____

SOURCE DATABASES: _____

SEARCH TERM DEVELOPMENT: _____

	CONNECTOR	TERM 2	CONNECTOR	TERM 3	CONNECTOR	TERM 4
TERM 1						

Primary _____

Alt. _____

Alt. _____

Alt. _____

Alt. _____

COMPLETED REQUEST: _____

RESULTS: _____

REVISED REQUEST: _____

RESULTS: _____

REVISED REQUEST: _____

RESULTS: _____

Fig. 7-3. Sample search planning form.

Chapter 8

Conversations with Information Brokers

I N THIS CHAPTER, YOU'LL MEET TWO WORKING INFORMATION BROKERS, FIND OUT HOW they see themselves, how they work, and what they see in the future. Their views and experiences can be helpful to you as you begin your business.

Carol and Bob Sherman operate Computer Assisted Research On Line (C.A.R.O.L.) from their home in Miami, from their office, or with a portable computer when travel is necessary. Chris Wesselman operates Research One from his "home office" in Dallas, Texas. The Shermans are generalists; Wesselman specializes in financial information, with a particular emphasis on mergers and acquisitions. Bob Sherman likes searching with his trusty Tandy Model 100; Chris Wesselman is a big fan of his Macintosh.

Getting Started

"In the progression from information to knowledge, one must remember what Einstein said: Imagination is more important than knowledge," Wesselman says. "You could set up a cot at the New York Library, but that wouldn't mean you would be informed. There's a lot of art to information. I've seen people at seminars who I know immediately would never be effective online searchers. Of course, I'd never tell them that."

Two things Chris Wesselman does tell beginners: information brokers must be information addicts. They must also be sales persons.

Wesselman remembers well when he first saw the term "information broker" in an article by Steve Roberts in "Online Today" magazine in the fall of 1982. He had purchased his first microcomputer in the fall in 1981 so he could access Dow Jones News/Retrieval as part of his work as a marketing executive for an oil company.

"I didn't even realize I was going to get word processing and spreadsheets and all the nifty things we have now. But that's how I actually got started. It was quite exciting the first time I logged on, and it's still fun today," he says.

He started with Dow Jones, signed onto The Source and CompuServe, and then DIALOG. By the beginning of 1983, he had become well-versed in these database services, but still had not begun to do research for anyone other than his employer and himself.

After reading the "Online Today" article, he sent his first electronic mail message to Roberts, saying, "You've put a name to what I want to do, what should I do next?" As is typical with electronic mail systems, the answer came the next day: "Call Learned Information and go to the Online Meeting in New York, April 1, 1983."

Wesselman called, went, and for the first time met people who were actively involved in the information industry. This was the beginning of his career as an information broker.

He admits he did "a lot of funny things" at first. It was a new field, a new career, and he missed out on some opportunities, such as a European symposium on information brokering.

"But then, I didn't have any rules. My first concern was hardware, and I'm afraid a lot of people still come at it from the hardware angle. This is unfortunate because, at this point, a Commodore 64 would work fine. Hardware isn't the problem," he says.

"But above and beyond the hardware, and even whatever software is being used, an information broker has to have the information flair, the proclivity, the interest. It is an art and a science.

"I spent easily $2,500–$3,000 before I felt anywhere near proficient on the system," he says, adding that online experience and training seminars offered by the database vendors are both important. "Once I made that kind of investment, I thought, well gee, this is interesting. Maybe I can do this for other people."

Marketing: The Make-or-Break Factor

But, of course, his next problem was marketing. No matter what aspect of the information brokering business he talks about, Wesselman ties it into marketing. In his opinion, a perfect information brokering company (which he describes in detail later) would have one person searching full time, one person analyzing data full time and at least one person, maybe two, marketing full time.

"I can't come back to that selling side enough, because it's critically important. All you have to do is pick up the want ads in any Sunday paper and look at the ratio of sales ads to everything else. At least 50 percent of the ads will be in sales. A friend of mine, a psychologist, says it really doesn't matter if you drop out of junior high school. If you can sell, you can succeed in this country," he says.

He estimates that in the information brokering business, 80 percent of the effective advertising is word of mouth, and the most asked question at gatherings of information brokers is "How do you market?"

As discussed in Chapter 3, the decision whether to specialize is an important part of your marketing. First, Wesselman says, because telling people you can do anything they want comes across as "strange, at best." Second, because specializing helps overcome marketing jitters.

"For someone who says, 'OK, I'm ready to go, what do I do now?' the answer is: 'Get clients,' " Wesselman says. "Get your sneakers on, get out there and start pounding pavement. It's something that's very hard for information-oriented people to do. But specializing will sharply reduce the number of people you have to call on cold."

Beginners often try to cover the entire market, believing the wealth and diversity of information accessible online makes them instant experts in virtually any subject. Wesselman says corporate searchers and librarians who have been doing online searching for 10 years or more may have the ability to "cover the waterfront," but they are exceptions, not the rule. Further, he says, specialization limits the amount of research you have to do just to keep yourself current.

Corporate Minds on the Bottom Line

Wesselman points out that corporate minds will be hard to convince when selling information services and products. They like to believe they can do without information, preferring to manage "by the seat of their pants."

"Someone at an Information Industry Association (IIA) meeting was talking about how she went to interview some very notable editor. This guy's office had stacks of papers all over the floor, all over everything. No shelves, just stacks. She says, 'How do you do all this research, any of it online?' He says, 'No, I can't afford all that, but I've got it all right here. It's all here somewhere.' "

This is the sort of attitude an aspiring information broker will encounter. Wesselman says business minds will answer a sales pitch with "How are you going to pay for yourself?" Be prepared for clients who want an instant, quantifiable answer to that question. If you can't justify yourself to them, they'll never be convinced to buy your service.

But even those who need information, and who realize it, may not know how much it is worth. Since information has been for so long perceived to be free, it is hard for a client to understand just looking for information costs money today. Wesselman tells the story of a search for a customer which turned up nothing. Wesselman felt he was being fair charging only his online costs of $100. The client tried to talk him down from that.

An information broker must realize, he says, that the client has conflicting views: "free" information (as in going to a public library to search it out himself) versus how much convenience is worth to him. The latter is worth a great deal to some people, as evidenced by convenience stores that feature fast service at high prices.

Chris Dobson knows some brokers who don't charge for searches that don't turn up any information and her reaction to that practice is quite clear:

> Remember that you're selling a service, *not* just information. Your database system contracts actually prohibit you from selling the information, in most cases. And since what you're selling is your services in locating and compiling whatever information is

available which meets the specifications, your clients should expect to pay for the time you spend even if there is little information available. In many cases, the fact that the information is *not* there is what the client needs to know. For instance, if we check the software databases for a particular application type to run on a VAX and don't find one, the software consultant we do the work for knows that there is no competition if he decides to market the one he has written. I actually know one broker who does not charge her clients when she is unable to find the information they want. *That is crazy.* You are selling your time, experience, and expertise. The client gets all the benefit of it whether you bury him in paper or tell him there's nothing out there. [Emphasis is hers.]

Expectations Mean a Lot

A great deal also depends on the customer's expectations of what the finished product will be. Wesselman feels the customer only wants the answer, not a pile of data to wade through. Analysis, however, and simple word processing performed on data to get it to readable form, takes valuable, and billable, time. Wesselman developed a three-tiered pricing system with different charges for raw data, edited data and analyzed data, taking into account the time each one involved.

"Information brokering fees will likely increase as the complexity of databases increase, simply because it's too time-consuming and inconvenient for clients to learn the newest stuff," he says.

On the subject of pricing, Wesselman suggests you double your online database costs as a guide to determine a fair rate for your client and lobby database vendors to institute a fee structure that rewards efficient searchers with discounts. He notes that many information brokers have minimum charges. His own minimum fee is $75 to $100; he knows other information brokers, mostly specialists, who have minimums of $300 or more.

"When you look at editing, invoicing, and collection problems, this work can be very time-consuming," he says. "I know people in Dallas who'll think nothing of charging $1,200–$2,000 for a search."

In summary, the Wesselman rules seem to be:

• Know your potential customers, and how much they are paying for information now.

• Know your costs, not only direct, online costs but the labor cost to polish the data into a finished product.

• Know what the client thinks you are selling: raw data, analyzed data, or the rough draft of his finished report. Charge accordingly.

Costs Are a Stumbling Block

"One of the major stumbling blocks in information brokering, any CPA will tell you, is that your direct expenses are so high. I've surveyed my records and found my online charges averaged between 43 and 62 percent of what I had billed. That's extremely high for a service industry. Your CPA would like to see it at a two-to-one ratio,'' Wesselman says. "This is difficult."

Some databases are prohibitively expensive. Wesselman pointed out that World Reporter has a list of all the imports and exports in the world, but the access fee is $6,000 a year. "The Tulsa File, an oil-industry data compilation run by the University of Oklahoma, costs $1,000 a year. Even corporations who need this information may find it hard to come up with that kind of money."

While some vendors charge more for using their system at higher baud rates, some charge the same rate, which is really "a price break for downloading," he points out. Wesselman lobbies for discounts because efficient searchers don't bog down the system, and that helps keep the vendors' other customers happier.

And then there are the manuals. "Some vendors—seeking profits, of course—are selective about distribution of their documentation by charging up to $100 each. Updates and revisions are frequent." Wesselman points to a large pile of manuals, revisions, updates and flyers from database vendors; a month's worth of them would take a week to read.

It's all part of the cost of being an information broker.

The Perfect Information Brokerage

Many information brokers start out as independent entrepreneurs. Only as sales and activity increase do they bring in more people. "As Sue Rugge has proved, you can build quite a large firm in information brokering," Wesselman says.

"One of the things I have pondered is how one would put together an information research company," Wesselman says. "Two factors work against it: Information-type people are very independent by nature. They don't easily ally together. And the client is usually very interested in confidentiality," which, of course, is harder to maintain with more employees.

Assuming these two issues can be settled, "It would be nice to have sort of a tag-team approach, where one person retrieves, another analyzes and one, or even two, market."

Even beyond that, he says, you could have specialized searchers. "Having one whose specialty is legal research, someone specializing in business research, someone else searching chemistry and biology, and so on, would help efficiency."

Informally, you can build such a "company," he suggests, by interacting with other information brokers, trading off jobs as subcontracts when asked to search something you don't feel you can handle.

Using this approach, "you can retrieve information from several different sources, some rather esoteric, in answering a client's question. Nevertheless, it's important to remember that the information must look consistent to the user," he says. "That's part of the service, and part of the charges, of course."

Issues and Conflicts in Information Brokering

Wesselman commented on several conflicts and issues within the information industry.

He notes the nature of access will change when information is widely available on CD-ROM. But several questions must be resolved. "Is this online access? Will it be cheaper? Will it be feasible for all types of information?"

Another conflict is between "experts" (ranging from librarians who have traditionally controlled access to information through expertise, to MIS types who control mainframes) and the new information professionals. The former worry that "amateurs in computer or information science shouldn't be messing with this new technology," Wesselman says. He sees this as "territorialism," and also notes that it is one thing keeping the information industry smaller than it might be otherwise.

Wesselman is concerned about maintaining the American lead in information technology. One way to ensure the lead is to keep using the electronic sources of information so the vendors can afford to stay in business, he says. However, this leads to another conflict that also reflects the territorialism just mentioned: bottlenecks are forming at times on the most useful database services. CD-ROMs and gateways may help the problem; superconductivity may also hold a key.

"Artificial intelligence (AI) as applied to online database searching may drastically change how research is conducted," Wesselman says. "Vendors may one day create true AI systems that point out the best files for the information you seek, or even select the file for you.

"All this technology is very new and, of course, predictions are made for reality to ignore," he says. "It remains to be seen just how much potential is realized."

C.A.R.O.L.

Though Carol Sherman is the president of Computer Assisted Research On Line, Inc. (C.A.R.O.L.), her husband and vice-president Bob Sherman is the able and articulate spokesman for the organization. He is not shy about expressing his opinions, his likes and dislikes.

"The worst part is the people who want it yesterday for $25," says Bob, "especially if I know I'll spend a couple of days on the search. Two days work is not worth $60. I have yet to do any search in which I put anywhere near the time online to what I put on preparation, so that I can get on and get off."

It All Began in Miami

For all their adult lives, he and his wife have been involved in research: Bob as a reporter and Carol as owner and operator of the largest private news service in the Southeast. Her service, started in 1974, serves radio and television stations, all major networks, and wire services. The couple became information brokers almost by accident.

"I became involved in computing in 1979 and became aware you could reach out and grab information," he says. "I began investigating what was out there. Others in the profession [journalism] started to show me a market."

Soon, he was conducting a wide variety of searches as favors for friends. In November 1982, he and Carol decided that the searches performed for friends could be a business, and so C.A.R.O.L. was formed. Their initial clients were those other journalists—friends and acquaintances who needed quick, reliable background information. To expand their business, they used brochures, free advertising, mass mailings, and word of mouth.

But from the first day, C.A.R.O.L. ran into a problem on the business management side: trying to become a credit card vendor.

"Thirteen banks flat-out turned me down immediately when they found out my business was telephone or mail order. In fact, that was their first question, then 'NO.' I was to the point of starting to think of a lawsuit against the largest bank in Miami, which started this policy," Bob says.

"I called the bank, asked to speak to the president, and said, 'You're the big guy, who do I sue in your organization?'

" 'Let's not get huffy,' he said, 'we'll work something out.' It was almost a month of daily hassles. They kept telling me horror stories about people using credit cards to burn merchants, using the credit protection laws. Finally, I posted $5,000 bond against charge-backs."

That major obstacle overcome, it became a matter of building on what they already knew to make the business a success.

Asked what preparation was necessary to be an information broker, Bob says, "My biggest asset is years of experience as a reporter, digging out things people don't want dug."

But, he and Carol had also laid good groundwork in experience and training on databases and services. They signed up for every database service they could find, took classes and read documentation.

Start-up Costs

The Shermans spent nearly $20,000 in equipment, sign-up fees, software, and tuition for various courses before they declared themselves to be in business.

The costs of operation didn't stop there, of course. For instance, in January 1984, one database service began to charge a $100/month minimum billing. The only alternative to that fee was to put up a large deposit to be held for 12 months.

"I wrote a letter protesting this, and got one back suggesting that I go in with four or five other small information brokers to share the minimum." It was a tough decision, he says, to forgo the database service, since "you don't know when you'll need that particular one." He sees hope in the fact that the vendor is being boycotted by universities and libraries because of that policy, which could cut their profits sharply.

Fees

The Sherman's price structure for a job depends on the customer. A repeat customer with a contract will get better rates than a one-time requestor, he says.

"Our fees haven't changed since the day we began," Bob says. "We base it on what we feel is a fair amount: So much per hour plus expenses. Although I always do more than an hour for homework on a search, I have yet to charge more than an hour for the search itself."

Because of the costs involved, Bob says C.A.R.O.L.'s policy is strictly prepayment.

"This can be in the form of a check in advance, a bank guarantee, credit card authorization, or whatever," he explained. His corporate clients, such as a nationwide private investigation company whose individual offices often call for research, will be billed, but that is part of the contract he has with them. For the smaller clients, prepayment and a verbal agreement for the search is the rule.

Four-Point Marketing System

C.A.R.O.L.'s clients include the major television networks, magazines and scriptwriters. It would have been very hard to gather that clientele without his contacts from his journalism work, Sherman says.

He has had success selling to major corporations, even though they have in-house research departments, for four main reasons:

- C.A.R.O.L. can be more cost effective than the client's keeping four or five employees waiting for requests for information. These salaried people can go on to other productive work.

- Sometimes Bob is used as supplemental help in a crunch. There are times when the in-house research people get swamped. Then C.A.R.O.L. might be used as a stringer for the R&D department.

- Bob can prove he is less expensive. "I put myself on a benchmark test against in-house people. Using custom software I wrote myself plus techniques I have learned, my search was more cost-effective, minute for minute, than the major R&D in-house operation," Bob says.

- Finally, because it is independent, C.A.R.O.L. is more efficient. Salaried persons are rarely in a hurry. Add to that the many courses and training, computerized routines, and techniques he uses, and Bob can serve the client better.

"And if you can't do better than they (the clients) can, you don't have a service to sell," he notes.

Generalists, Not Specialists

Because of their wide background in researching for news, the Shermans are not specializing at this time as to which subjects they search. They do specialize, however, in the type of product they deliver.

"Most of those who do business only in a local area are usually heavily involved in actual document delivery," Bob noted. That is not a service C.A.R.O.L. offers. They do current awareness, regular searches with SDI or instant education on a subject.

"Most of our clients are looking for specific information, not necessarily the actual document. We do have associates across the country who do document retrieval for us on a retainer basis," he says.

They Are Not Alone

C.A.R.O.L. uses associates for time-intensive searches, or searches that take advantage of the associates' specialties.

If a search can be done without a computer, Bob says he reports that to the client, and suggests where the client should go for the information. "I don't feel right taking money if I can't do the job," he says.

He has also been in time situations that made him send the client to another information broker, or to stringers with experience in library sciences.

"What you get on the computer is a small part of what needs to be done," he points out. "The hard part is to find out what the customer wants to know."

Bob says the key to success in information brokering is that ability to determine the exact nature of the information need, structure the search properly, and know which database to use and how to use it well.

In fact, that is why he likes his stringers to have research experience, which is as important as computer skills in his opinion. Each of the stringers has a special ability: one specializes in certain databases, another is good at general clerical duties.

Training and Training

"My biggest asset is many years of knowing how and when to obtain information," he says. "All my adult life I've been trained to get results, ferreting our what people didn't want ferreted out. How to ask the same question 16 different ways. Not to take 'No' for an answer.

"I look back at my last 30 years in the news business where I was constantly taught and trained how to ask questions, and how to 'read between the lines' and pursue answers . . . . without it I'd be lost."

It especially helps if you get a question such as: "How does weather affect behavior?"—Sherman's favorite example of a vague search request you shouldn't accept. He had to ask a lot of questions of that client before he could begin, he says.

Meanwhile the quest for better and more training and information continues. "Documentation to the databases is expensive, but necessary to cut online costs," he says. "The medical thesaurus on DIALOG is an example. By itself it cost more than $275. The controlled vocabulary is tremendous. Without it, you may get lucky, and an abstract will have your term, but the medical vocabulary is the key to an efficient search. You need four or five other manuals as well, just to keep up. Information providers to DIALOG have such manuals for sale and they are worth it rather than going on unprepared."

He also recommends going to all courses and classes offered by database publishers and vendors. Since they often offer one-on-one exchanges, they allow for a lot of question-and-answer time.

Noting that several software houses now offer search aid programs, he warns that the amount of disk space and memory they require may be prohibitive.

Training in programming might help, too, but is not essential, Bob says. "Programming is not necessary to do an information search. The number one technique is to know how to get in, do it right, and get out."

"The best thing is to have good communications software that will speed up your online work, to keep reading the latest documentation on the systems you use and to use the databases often. Every database has its own methods, indices, codes, and so on. If you don't know the control codes for a subject you may wander and drift for a long time."

Advice for Fledglings

Asked for advice for those just beginning in the information brokering business, Bob had several comments.

"It's not something you can start on a shoestring, if you do it properly," he says. "It's not a gravy train. Every time our business turns a profit, we put it back into the business."

He hits hard on that subject because he is concerned about some newer information brokers. "I'm concerned with people prostituting the business. We're starting to see people who think information brokering is a quick way to make a buck," Bob says. "We all suffer for the kids who are playing around. Bad brokers are bad for the field. I'm concerned about it. If you just don't care about your product, you're not going to find the rewards."

Bob says it's hard to define your equipment needs, except in a general way. "You need a terminal or computer, a good quality printer, lots of storage, and of course, a modem.

"I can't say that I would recommend any one, two or three databases. We belong to [almost] every database service we have ever heard about. Some we have never used apart from taking training on their use. But a good broker must be willing to make this investment because one never knows when the question will come along that will require some obscure service's use. We do try to avoid the services that attempt to impose monthly minimum charges.''

He warns that he has had ''a lot of hassles'' since the first day C.A.R.O.L. existed. ''The first thing I realized is that in order to make this work for payment, deadlines are important: Get searches done quickly.

''The best part about this business is that it helps me to see a never-ending quest to learn come true. I learn, too. I see every report before it goes out. I rank that with my experience spending time with royalty and Presidents as a reporter (for *Life* magazine) and seeing life in the barrios and ghettos as a way to increase learning ability,'' he said.

For his final words of wisdom, Bob Sherman quotes what his father taught him: ''If you're going to do it, do it right. If you're not going to do it right, don't do it at all.''

Now that you know how these two brokers did it, it's just about time for you to do it, too. All that remains is the tool kit.

Chapter 9

Resources

ASA SELF-EMPLOYED PROFESSIONAL OR SMALL BUSINESS OWNER, YOU ARE GOING TO
have to do all you can to maintain your competitive advantages and to minimize your
competitive weaknesses. One of the ways you can do this is through participation in
the larger community of professional information brokers. Since this is a fairly new field,
there are not too many associations for you to join, nor much press about this particular
discipline. However, many resources are available to you, and, if you are to be successful,
you need to be aware of some of them and to take advantage of at least a few of them.

In this chapter, you are going to learn of some of the resources available to you.
Included will be online database services, books, periodicals, associations, articles, etc.
You need not use each and every resource mentioned here; this is intended to give you
an understanding of the kind of support available to you. Look over the list, investigate
what interests you, and remain alert to new resources as they become available or as
you discover them.

As you gain experience as an information broker, you will develop preferences for
certain associations, sources and events. You will begin to develop your own custom
version of this resource list, and you may have but a few items from this list on yours.
You can begin with this list, however, and build on it, subtract from it, and change it
to fit your needs.

Send for more information on these resources using the addresses and phone numbers
provided. Do your own research and feel free to disagree with whatever you please.
But do explore some of these resources. They will provide you with a sense of perspective
and help you understand that you are not alone in what you do. That reassurance is of
particular importance to those of you who will be working alone and/or working from home.

One caveat: Names, addresses and phone numbers change, particularly in areas such as information and publishing. Therefore, some of what follows may be out of date by the time you read it. Follow through and you'll get to the people you're seeking.

Online Database Services

If you're fairly new to the world of online information, you may be unaware of the full range of electronic information resources available to you. The number of database vendors, and the number of databases, may surprise you. And when you stop to consider that these database services are only one aspect of the information industry, you should begin to appreciate the scope of the task you have set for yourself.

The database services included here are not examined critically. There is simply too much variety, both in the services themselves and in the uses you might make of them, to offer any recommendations of what is best for you. Instead, write or call those services that interest you and request full information on their services. Decide for yourself which services will be right for you. Don't just assume you need every resource mentioned here, and don't think you can get very far with only one source of information. Your information resources must be custom matched to your information needs.

Most database vendors, and many database publishers, offer specific training in the use of their product or service, and you should take that training for the databases and services you plan to use. This is an important part of your training, not only in the operation and use of a specific database or service, but in the workings of the information industry, as well. You might be disappointed by the cost of some of the training, but if you're to make the best use of these services, that training is indispensable.

ADP Network Services
Automatic Data Processing, Inc.
175 Jackson Plaza
Ann Arbor, MI 48106
(800) 521-3166
(313) 769-6800

BRS/SEARCH, BRS/BRKTHRU, and BRS/After Dark
BRS Information Technologies
1200 Route 7
Latham, NY 12110
(800) 227-5277
(518) 783-7251

Data Resources
Data Resources, Inc.
24 Hartwell Ave.
Lexington, MA 02173
(617) 863-5100

DataTimes

DataTimes
Suite 450, Parkway Plaza
14000 Quail Springs Parkway
Oklahoma City , OK 73134
(800) 642–2525
(405) 751–6400

DIALOG, Knowledge Index, and DIALMAIL

DIALOG Information Services
3460 Hillview Avenue
Palo Alto, CA 94304
(800) 334–2564
(415) 858–3719

Dow Jones News/Retrieval

Dow Jones News/Retrieval Service
P.O. Box 300
Princeton, NJ 08540
(800) 522–3567
(609) 452–2000

EasyNet

Telebase Systems, Inc.
763 W. Lancaster Ave.
Bryn Mawr, PA 19010
(215) 526–2800

InfoService and InfoMagic

I.P. Sharp Associates, Inc.
Suite 1900
2 First Canadian Place
Toronto M5X 1E3
Canada
(800) 387–1588
(416) 364–5361

LEXIS, MEDIS, and NEXIS

Mead Data Central
P.O. Box 933
Dayton, OH 45401
(800) 227–4908
(513) 865–6800

NewsNet
NewsNet, Inc.
945 Haverford Road
Bryn Mawr, PA 19010
(800) 345–1301
(215) 527–8030

ORBIT Search Service and Pergamon Infoline
Pergamon ORBIT Infoline
1340 Old Chain Bridge Road
McLean, VA 22101
(800) 421–7229
(703) 442–0900

QL Search
QL Systems Ltd.
Suite 1018, Tower B
112 Kent Street
Ottawa, Ontario K1P 5P2
Canada
(613) 238–3499

VU/TEXT
VU/TEXT Information Services, Inc.
1211 Chestnut St.
Philadelphia, PA 19107
(800) 258–8080
(215) 665–3300

WESTLAW
West Publishing Co.
50 W. Kellog Blvd.
St. Paul, MN 55165
(800) 328–9833
(612) 228–2692

Wilsonline
H. W. Wilson Co.
950 University Ave.
Bronx, NY 10452
(800) 367–6770
(212) 588–8400

Other Online Services

CompuServe Information Service, Inc.
5000 Arlington Centre Blvd.
Columbus, OH 43220
(800) 848–8990
(614) 457–8650

Genie
General Electric Information Services
401 N. Washington St.
Rockville, MD 20850
(301) 340–4000

MCI Mail
1133 19th St., N.W.
Washington, DC 20036
(202) 872–1600

The Source
Source Telecomputing Corp.
1616 Anderson Road
McLean, VA 22102
(800) 336–3330
(703) 821–8888

Other Information Resources

These resources, primarily manufacturers and distributors of CD-ROM products, are involved in a volatile area, and changes in companies, products and services will certainly take place. Here, more than any other area in this chapter, you must do some homework and seek out the information you need from any of these companies. But some of these products and services will survive and be important parts of the information industry of the future, so this list is worth including, no matter how fast it might change.

Compact Disclosure
Disclosure Information Group
5161 River Road
Bethesda, MD 20816
(301) 951–1300

CD/Corporate and CD/CorpTech
Datext, Inc.
444 Washington St.
Woburn, MA 01801
(617) 938–6667

One Source
Lotus Development Corp.
55 Cambridge Parkway
Cambridge, MA 02142
(617) 577–8500

PC Plus
Standard & Poor's Compustat
7400 S. Alton Ct.
Englewood, CO 80112
(800) 525–8640

Grolier Electronic Encyclopedia
Grolier Electronic Publishing
95 Madison Ave., Suite 1100
New York, NY 10016
(212) 696–9750

Books in Print and Ulrich's International Periodical Index
R.R. Bowker Co.
205 E. 42nd St.
New York, NY 10017
(800) 323–3288
(212) 916–1605

Wilsondisc
H.W. Wilson Co.
950 University Ave.
Bronx, NY 10452
(800) 367–6770
(212) 588–2266

ERIC
DIALOG Information Services
3460 Hillview Avenue
Palo Alto, CA 94304
(800) 334–2564
(415) 858–3719

Magazines and Newsletters

In a field that is changing as rapidly as information brokering, no single book could provide you with all of the up-to-date information you need. New programs, databases, resources, etc., are entering the market daily, and you need to know what these developments are. Subscribing to a number of periodicals in the trade press is an excellent way to stay current, and you will get a sampling of what is available. One very nice thing about these resources is that each and every one will not only serve as a resource, but will lead you on to other resources as well. Please note that some publishers have more than one publication. When that is the case, all publications are listed in a single record.

AIM Network
Associated Information Managers
1776 E. Jefferson St.
Rockville, MD 20852
(301) 231-7447

Access: Microcomputers in Libraries
DAC Publications
3354 30th St.
San Diego, CA 92104

Advanced Technology/Libraries
Knowledge Industry Publications, Inc.
701 Westchester Ave.
White Plains, NY 10604
(800) 248-5474
(914) 328-9157

DLA Bulletin
University of California
Division of Library Automation
186 University Hall
Berkeley, CA 94720
(415) 642-9485

DATABASE, ONLINE, and The Laserdisk Professional
Online, Inc.
11 Tannery Lane
Weston, CT 06883
(203) 227-8466

Database Searcher
    Meckler Publishing
    11 Ferry Lane W.
    Westport, CT 06880
    (203) 226–6967

Electronic Library, Electronic and Optical Publishing Review, Information Today, LINK-UP, and Online Review
    Learned Information, Inc.
    143 Old Marlton Pike
    Medford, NJ 08055
    (609) 654–6266

Infomediary
    Elsevier Science Publishers
    P.O. Box 211
    1000 AE Amsterdam, Netherlands

Information Broker
    Burwell Enterprises
    5106 FM 1960 W., Suite 349
    Houston, TX 77069
    (713) 537–9051

Information Technology and Libraries, LITA Newsletter, and Library Systems Newsletter
    American Library Association
    50 E. Huron St.
    Chicago, IL 60611
    (312) 944–6780

Information Times
    Information Industry Association
    555 New Jersey Ave., N.W., Suite 800
    Washington, DC 20001
    (202) 639–8262

Journal of the American Society for Information Science
    American Society for Information Science
    c/o John Wiley & Sons
    605 Third Avenue
    New York, NY 10016
    (212) 850–6000

Library Hi-Tech News
Pierian Press
P.O. Box 1808
Ann Arbor, MI 48106
(313) 434–6409

Wired Librarian's Newsletter
Micro Libraries
No. 2C Andover Dr.
Athens, OH 45702
or
20 Congress Ave.
   Sioux City, IA 51104
   (614) 594–7757

Reference Books

As noted earlier, it is difficult, at best, for any book to be the only resource an information broker will ever need. You will find other books that are of interest to you as you continue your work. What is offered here is not, by any means, an exhaustive list, but books you ought to consider. Also, you should watch the trade press for news of additional books.

The Computer Data and Database Source Book by Matthew Lesko is a good resource for the information broker in that it is a comprehensive list of data sources. It may be a little out of date (though subsequent editions should keep that in check), but most of the resources given will remain valid for some time to come. The book is colored by Mr. Lesko's contagious enthusiasm for information and the information industry. For more information, contact:

Avon Books
1790 Broadway
New York, NY 10019
(212) 399–1357

Computer-Readable Data Bases: A Directory and Data Sourcebook is a biennial publication concentrating on U. S. databases that are publicly and/or commercially available and includes names and addresses, services and fees charged. For more information, contact:

American Society for Information Science
1010 16th Street, N.W.
Washington, DC 20036
(202) 659–3644

Data Bases for Business: Profiles & Applications by Van Mayros and D. Michael Werner was published in 1982 and, as such, may be more out of date than the others. It contains more detailed information about information brokering, however, including a list of major brokers and an examination of services that an information broker might offer. It's a good getting-started book. For more information, contact:

Chilton Book Company
Radnor, PA 19089
(215) 964–4743

Databasics: Your Guide to Online Business Information by Doran Howitt and Marvin I. Weinberger is a good book for anyone considering going online, as it offers a background on the electronic information industry and an in-depth examination of several database producers, online systems, software and hardware. For more information, contact:

Garland Publishing
136 Madison Avenue
New York, NY 10016

Datapro Directory of On-line Services from Datapro Research Corporation (a McGraw-Hill Co.) is by far the most comprehensive directory of databases, database vendors and information services available. It is also priced accordingly. Much of the information contained in the two three-ring binders is readily available from the individual companies and vendors, but to have it conveniently cross-indexed and cross-referenced and in one neat and usable package may be worth the healthy annual subscription price. Certainly, for any serious information broker, it is worth the $30 to review the directory for 30 days. For more information, contact:

Datapro Research Corporation
1805 Underwood Blvd.
P.O. Box 1066
Delran, NJ 08075
(609) 764–0100

Directory of Fee–Based Information Services, edited by Helen Burwell, lists a great number of information services and information brokers in both the United States and Canada. It's always good to know who's who in your field so you can network when necessary and position yourself in relation to the rest of the industry. Look for annual editions. For more information, contact:

Burwell Enterprises
5106 F.M. 1960 W., Suite 349
Houston, TX 77069
(713) 537–9051

Directory of Online Databases is a quarterly publication that basically is a list of databases available online, giving some pricing, availability, and scope information about each database. Because this directory is updated quarterly, it is more current than directories published in book form. The databases are listed alphabetically, but there is a subject index to help you find the database you need. For more information, contact:

Cuadra/Elsevier
P.O. Box 1672
Grand Central Station
New York, NY 10163
(212) 916–1010
(212) 916–1180

Encyclopedia of Information Systems and Services—an international guide to computer-readable databases, database producers and publishers, online vendors and time-sharing companies, telecommunications networks, videotext/teletext systems, information retrieval software, library and information networks, bibliographic utilities, library management systems, fee-based information services, data collection and analysis centers, community information and referral systems, consultants and service companies, associations, clearinghouses, and research centers. Edited by Anthony T. Kruzas and John Schmittroth, Jr. For more information, contact:

Gale Research Company
Book Tower
Detroit, MI 48226
(313) 961–2242

Fee-Based Information Services: A Study of a Growing Industry by Richard W. Boss and Lorig Maranjian is one of a series of books on information management from Bowker. While it was published in 1980, the book does provide some valuable information about what information brokers were doing in the areas of management and marketing, as well as research. For more information, contact:

R.R. Bowker Co.
205 E. 42nd St.
New York, NY 10017
(800) 323–3288
(212) 916–1727

How to Look it Up Online: Get the Information Edge with Your Personal Computer by Alfred Glossbrenner is a book that attempts the impossible with a great deal of success. This is a very comprehensive overview of the online information world that would be a first-rate complement to this book. For more information, contact:

The Rugge Group
1626 Chestnut St.
Berkeley, CA 94702
(415) 524-3212

How To Win With Information or Lose Without It, by Andrew P. Gavin and Hubert Bermont, is an excellent treatment of the problem of not knowing the value of information, how to ask for it, how to acquire it and how to manage it. While it may not help your online search technique, this book will help you understand the problems your clients face and help you help them deal with those problems. That, in turn, will make you a better information broker. For more information, contact:

Bermont Books
815 15th St., N.W.
Washington, DC 20005

The Independent Scholar's Handbook: How to Turn Your Interest in Any Subject Into Expertise by Ronald Gross, is a guide to research that may be useful to information brokers possessing expertise in a particular discipline but not in research techniques. For more information, contact:

Addison-Wesley Publishing Co., Inc.
Jacob Way
Reading, MA 01867

The Information Brokers: How to Start & Operate Your Own Fee-Based Service by Kelly Warnken is another step-by-step approach to getting started as an information broker. This book, while directed primarily at library science professionals, contains a lot of good, basic information. For more information, contact:

The Rugge Group
1626 Chestnut St.
Berkeley, CA 94702
(415) 524-3212

Inside Information: Business and Professional Electronic Libraries, Databases and Messaging by John Helliwell is written for the business or professional person who is interested in gaining access to online databases for personal use—the "end user." It is an excellent introduction to the online world with enough basic information for the beginner and enough richness for the more advanced searcher. For more information, contact:

New American Library
1633 Broadway
New York, NY 10019

Mind Your Own Business: A Guide for the Information Entrepreneur by Alice Sizer Warner draws on Warner's extensive experience in the information industry (she was a founder of Warner-Eddison Associates in 1973). There is a definite instructional tone to the book, which is appropriate as it is an outgrowth of a course of the same name Warner taught. For more information, contact:

The Rugge Group
1626 Chestnut St.
Berkeley, CA 94702
(414) 524-3212

Answers Online by Barbara Newlin is a tutorial that explains exactly what you do when you sit in front of the terminal and go online. It's written by Information on Demand's former Director of Research. For more information, contact:

The Rugge Group
1626 Chestnut St.
Berkeley, CA 94702
(415) 524-3212

So You Want to Be an Information Broker?, edited by Kelly Warnken and Barbara Felicetti, is a transcript of a conference held in 1982 at State University of New York in Albany. This booklet features the comments of several active participants in the information field. For more information, contact:

Information Alternative
P.O. Box 657
Woodstock, NY 12498

Professional Associations

Association with one's peers, with the opportunity to exchange information, resources, horror stories, and humor, is an important resource. Several organizations have been formed to support, oppose, consider, discuss, and work in areas of concern to the information broker. Here is a list of several you should consider. If you don't join, perhaps you can at least get on the mailing list, look at a publications list, subscribe to a newsletter, attend a convention, or otherwise tap into the networks provided by these associations.

Ad Hoc Committee on Copyright Law (AHCCL)
c/o Dr. August W. Steinhilber
National School Boards Association
1055 Thomas Jefferson St., N.W.
Washington, D.C. 20007
(202) 337-7666

American Library Association
  50 E. Huron St.
  Chicago, IL 60611
  (312) 944-6780

American Society for Information Science (ASIS)
  Suite 204
  1424 16th St., N.W.
  Washington, D.C. 20036
  (202) 462-1000

Association of Independent Information Professionals
  Roberta Brody
  Membership, AIIP
  c/o Brody Information Services, Inc.
  9 Hillcrest Road
  Port Washington, NY 11050
  (516) 997-6546

Center for Research Libraries
  5721 Cottage Grove Avenue
  Chicago, IL 60637
  (312) 955-4545

Copyright Clearance Center
  21 Congress Street
  Salem, MA 01970
  (617) 744-3350

Information Industry Association (IIA)
  555 New Jersey Avenue, N.W.
  Suite 800
  Washington, D.C. 20001
  (202) 639-8262

National Commission on Libraries and Information Science (NCLIS)
  General Services Administration Building
  Suite 3122, 7th & D Streets, S.W.
  Washington, D.C. 20024
  (202) 382-0840

National Federation of Abstracting and Information Services (NFAIS)
112 S. 16th Street
Philadelphia, PA 19102
(215) 563–2406

Special Libraries Association
1700 18th St., NW
Washington, D.C. 20009
(202) 234–4700

Software

In the interview with Bob Sherman of C.A.R.O.L., Bob noted that the software he has developed gives him a real edge in search efficiency. While Bob won't reveal his secret here, this will alert you to some new software that has come to market to help online researchers do more in less time. Look for more software of this type, both discipline-specific and general, for a growing number of databases and hardware configurations.

Biblio-Link, Pro-Cite, and Pro-Search
Personal Bibliographic Software, Inc.
P.O. Box 4250
Ann Arbor, MI 48106
(313) 996–1580

DIALOGLINK
DIALOG Information Services, Inc.
3460 Hillview Ave.
Palo Alto, CA 94304
(800) 334–2564
(415) 858–3810

Micro-CSIN
CSIN User Service Office
BBN Laboratories, Inc.
300 N. 17th St.
Arlington, VA 22209
(703) 524–4870

Q-Base and Search Works
> Online Research Systems, Inc.
> 627 W. 113th St., Suite 4F
> New York, NY 10025
> (212) 408–3311

Sci-Mate Editor, Sci-Mate Manager, and Sci-Mate Searcher
> Institute for Scientific Information, Inc.
> 3501 Market Street
> Philadelphia, PA 19104

Search Helper
> Information Access Co.
> 11 Davis Dr.
> Belmont, CA 94002
> (800) 227–8431
> (415) 591–2333

SEARCHWARE
> Searchware, Inc.
> Suite E
> 22458 Ventura Blvd.
> Woodland Hills, CA 91364
> (818) 992–4325

Other Resources

Any independent professional needs to take advantage of available resources to improve his or her ability to compete, grow and function effectively. These resources include professional associations, seminars and workshops, and networks. In addition to the material provided elsewhere in this section, you should be aware of a few of the other kinds of resources that might be of use to an information broker.

"How to Make Money Doing Research With Your Computer," an interview with Sue Rugge, former president and founder of Information on Demand, conducted by Paul and Sarah Edwards. Good advice from one of the first and one of the most successful information brokers. Consists of two audio cassette tapes and is also available in paperback. For more information, contact:

> Sue Rugge
> 1626 Chestnut
> Berkeley, CA 94702
> (415) 524-3212

The Online Searcher's Rosetta Stone is a wall chart covering more than 25 commands on 11 different database systems so that you can quickly find out how to exit, leave, quit, logoff or disconnect from the online system you are using. For more information, contact:

Library at INFOMART
1950 Stemmons Freeway
Dallas, TX 75207

For those of you who are interested in learning more about the business of information brokering, John Everett, co-author of *Information for Sale: How to Start and Operate Your Own Data Research Service*, offers seminars on information brokering and is available for one-on-one consulting. You can reach him online via DIALMAIL (his ID# is 18847), or CompuServe (75525,1144), or you can write him at:

Response Time
Suite 0-69
314 MacArthur Commons
Irving, TX 75062

Additional Reading

What follows is a brief list of articles and papers that would make interesting reading for an information broker. Most will be readily available through any large library or a document delivery service. You don't have to read every one, though you ought to look up a few. In any case, this survey of what is being written will give you a better perspective for starting or continuing your work as an information broker. Pay attention to the publication date of this material because some resources may be too old to be relevant to your work. Don't discount an article *just* because it is a little old, though. Some wear better than others.

"AI's INFOSOURCE: What Started as Pilot Program is Now Corporate Subsidiary," by Gary Bratton and Beth Gibber. *Online* (Weston, Conn.), v. 6, pp. 25–27, November 1982.

"Barbara Whyte Felicetti: Confessions of an Information Broker," by Tom Surprenant. *Library Hi Tech*, 2 (3), p. 119, 1984.

"Brokers Filling Businesses' Information Gaps." *Marketing News*, v. 19, n. 21, p. 3, October 11, 1985.

"Business Information Sources and Statistics (Information for Management: Services and Sources)." *Management Decision*, v. 24, p. 64, March 1986.

"Communication in the Online Industry: How an Information Broker Uses Electronic Mail," by Libby Trudell. *Online* (Weston, Conn.), v. 7, pp. 60–64, November 1983.

"Computer Age Information Brokers." *Administrative Management*, v. 47, p. 6, April 1986.

"Corporate Use of CD-ROMs to Distribute Custom Databases Could Rise Dramatically," by Susan Janus. *PC Week*, v. 4, p. 110, June 23, 1987.

"Data Bases Speed the Decision-Making Process," by David Steinbrecher. *Word Processing & Information Systems*, pp. 33–40, January 1982.

"Data-power to the People; CD-ROM Gives Statistical Research Power to All Libraries and Challenges Librarians to Produce Answers, Not Sources," by James R. Kuhlman and Everett S. Lee. *American Libraries*, v. 17, p. 757, November 1986.

"Database History: From Dinosaurs to Compact Discs," by Lynne M. Neufeld and Martha Cornog. *Journal of the American Society for Information Science*, v. 37, p. 183, July 1986.

"Dial Mike for Answers Anytime, Any Subject," by Dick Kimmins. *Business First Columbus*, p. 1, December 24, 1984.

"Document Delivery," by Antoinette Walton Colbert. *Online* (Weston, Conn.), vol. 7, pp. 74–76, May 1983.

"Downloading and Uploading in Online Information Retrieval," by Alison Jameson. *Library Management* (U.K.), v. 8, n. 1, p. 1, 1987.

Drill and Practice Program for Online Retrieval, A," by B.R. Boyce, D. Martin, B. Francis and M.E. Slever. *Journal of the American Society for Information Science*, v. 35, p. 129, March 1984.

"EARS: An Online Bibliographic Search and Retrieval System Based on Ordered Explosion," by R. Ramesh and G. Drury-Colin. *Information Processing and Management* (U.K.), v. 23, n. 3, p. 225, 1987.

"Easy Data System Chosen for Datapoint Automation." *Library Journal* (LIBJA), p. 312, February 15, 1984.

"Electronic Information Services Deliver Data to Your Desktop," by Rick Minicucci. *Today's Office*, v. 22, n. 1, p. 56, June 1987.

"Entrepreneurial Explosion, The," by K. Mark. *Canadian Business*, v. 56, n. 11, p. 86, November 1983.

"Establishing a Business: Fundamental Aspects for Information Practitioners," by James A. Leach and Lynda Nash Leach. *Library Trends* (LIBTA), p. 327, Winter 1984.

"External Information Services: A Survey of Behavioral Aspects of Demand," by L.B. Methlie and A.M. Tverstol. *Information Management*, v. 5, n. 4–5, p. 269, September 1982.

"Fee-Based Information Services," by Susan Klement. *Special Libraries*, v. 72, 185(2), April 1981.

"FIND/SVP Does Your Research for You," by C.R. Riggs. *Dun & Bradstreet Reports*, v. 22, n. 1, pp. 32–33, January/February 1984.

"Future of Information Brokers in Europe, The" (book reviews). *Special Libraries* (SPLBA), p. 316, July 1983.

"Get in Touch with Those Public Databases," by Brendan Walsh. *Accountancy* (UK), v. 99, n. 1124, p. 137, April 1987.

"How Good an Online Searcher Are You? Twenty Questions About Medline, " by Susan J. Feinglos. *Online*, v. 11, p. 63, July 1987.

"How Information on Demand, a Profit-Making Information Broker, Contracted with the North Suburban Library System, a Public Library System, To Answer: The 200 Questions," by Barbara Newlin. *Library Journal*, v. 107, 151(3), January 15, 1982.

"How to Cure Information Paralysis," by Andrew P. Gavin and Hubert Bermont. *Marketing Times*, p. 37–41, May/June 1982.

"How to Use Electronic Data Bases," by I. Sager. *D&B Reports*, v. 22, p. 48, January/February 1984.

"Info Entrepreneurs, The," by Howard Fineman. *Newsweek* (NWSKA), p. 58, November 11, 1985.

"Information Access Comes of Age with Online Data Bases," by Patricia Teets. *Personnel Journal*, v. 60, p. 112, January 1987.

"Information Brokers," (corporate use of computer-based researchers), by Eric Freedman. *PC Week*, v. 3, p. 53, February 18, 1986.

Information Brokers and the Information by the Brokers (Az Informaciok Koezvetitoei es a Koezvetitoek Informacioi), by Peter Hegedues and Figyeloe Koenyvtari. 30(3) p. 260, 1984.

"Information Brokers Thrive by Helping Firms Get Facts," by Amal Nag. *Wall Street Journal*, section 2, p. 23 (Western edition), p. 31 (Eastern edition), July 7, 1981.

"Information Brokers," by B.M. Gupta, R. Kundra and S.P. Gupta. *Annals of Library Science and Documentation*, 30(2), pp. 63–73.

"Information Brokers: An Attempted Definition (Les Bibliotecaires-Conseils: Essai de Definition)," by Peirrette Bergeron, Johanne Guevremont and France Pontbriand. *Argus*, 14(2) p. 35, June 1985.

Information Brokers: Complement or Replacement?" by Blaise Cronin and Dennis Lewis. *Australian Special Libraries News*, 16(1), p. 30, June 1985.

"Information Brokers: Finding the Facts Business Needs," by Teri Flynn. *Business America*, v. 8, inside front cover, December 23, 1985.

"Information Brokers: New Breed with Access to Secondary Research" (marketing research services), by Carol Tanzer Johnson. *Marketing News*, v. 21, p. 14, February 27, 1987.

"Information Brokers: Service of the Information Age" (book excerpt), by John H. Everett and Elizabeth Powell Crowe. *Credit & Financial Management*, v. 87, p. 20, January/February 1985.

"Information Brokers: Tapping the Mother Lode." *Journal of Accountancy*, v. 159, p. 137, June 1985.

"Information Brokers: The Indispensable Service." *Business* (Atlanta, Ga.), v. 35, p. 58, July/August/September 1985.

"Information Liability: New Interpretations for Electronic Publishing," by Blodwen Tarter. *Online* (Weston, Conn.), v. 10, p. 61, September 1986.

"Information Practice and Malpractice . . . Do We Need Malpractice Insurance," by Anne P. Mintz. *Online*, 8(4), p. 20, July 1984.

"Information Practice and Malpractice," by Anne P. Mintz. *Library Journal*, 110 (15), p. 38, September 1985.

"Information Resources Specialist as Group Facilitator in an Organizational Setting, The," by Sara Galligan. *Special Libraries* (SPLBA), p. 246, Fall 1985.

"Information Sources Constituting the Management Literature (Information for Management: Services and Sources)." *Management Decision*, v. 24, p. 38, March 1986.

"Information, Please, is Business for Broker" (company profile), by Bradshaw Hovey, *Business First of Buffalo*, v. 2, p. 1, September 1, 1986.

"Intermediaries," by Carol Karolow. National Online Meeting Proceedings 1985: New York, p. 251, April 30–May 2, 1985.

"Investigation of Online Searcher Traits and Their Relationship to Search Outcome, An," by Trudi Bellardo. *Journal of the American Society for Information Science*, v. 36, p. 241, July 1985.

"Kathy Ackerman: Information Broker," by Nancy Arnott. *Executive Female*, v. 9, p. 44, January/February 1986.

"Knowledge Services Open the Door to Information," by David L. Farkas. *Modern Office Technology*, pp. 70–78, October 1983.

"Libraries in the Year 2010: The Information Brokers," by S.D. Neill. *Futurist*, pp. 47–51, October 1981.

"Living Databases for Online Professionals," by Mick O'Leary. *Online* (Weston, Conn.), v. 11, p. 6, March 1987.

"Many Different Types of Sources of Information, The," by Michael Asner. *Computing Canada*, v. 13, n. 12, p. 12, June 11, 1987.

"Marketing Electronic Information," by Lizzie Davenport and Blaise Cronin, *Online Review*, v. 11, p. 39, February 1987.

"Marketing Intermediary as an Information Seller: A New Approach, The," by Michael Etgar and Pinhas Zusman. *The Journal of Business* (Chicago), v. 55, p. 505, October 1982.

"Mead Data Central and 'All the News That's Fit to Print,' " by Maureen Corcoran. *Online*, p. 32(4), July 1983.

"Model for the Stopping Behavior of Users of Online Systems, A," by Paul B. Kantor. *Journal of the American Society for Information Science*, v. 38, p. 211, May 1987.

"New Emphasis on Information-Strategic Use and Brokers are Recommended." *Marketing News*, v. 20, p. 15, May 23, 1986.

"Observations of End-User Online Searching Behavior Over Eleven Years," by Winifred Sewell and Sandra Teitelbaum. *Journal of the American Society for Information Science*, v. 37, p. 234, July 1986.

"On Demand Information Service in Europe and the Information Broker Business in the United States: Changes in the Mode of Business of Information Service Activities" (In Japanese), by A. Joho Kanri Togawa. *Journal of Information Processing and Management*, 24(3), p. 204, 1981.

"One-Thousand Dollar Alternative: How One University Structures a Fee-Based Information Service for Local Industry, The," by Susan A. Cady and Berry G. Richards. *American Libraries*, v. 14, 175(2), March 1982.

"On-Line Information Retrieval Aids New Product Development," by Giovanni Binetti. *Industrial Marketing Management*, pp. 247–251, July 1980.

"Online Databases: Some Questions of Ownership," by Sally Drew. *Wilson Library Bulletin* (WLBUA), p. 661, June 1985.

"Online Optical Disk: Database Distribution Strategies," by Andrew D. Roscoe and Philip M. Parker. *Inform*, v. 1, n. 5, p. 12, May 1987.

"Online Searching Styles: A Case-Study-Based Model of Searching Behavior," by R. Fidel. *Journal of the American Society for Information Science*, v. 35, n. 34, p. 211, July 1984.

"Online Services, Information Technology, and the Information Industry in Europe," by Jacky Deunnette. *Online*, v. 11, p. 121, July 1987.

"Online Views on Costs and Cost-Effectiveness," by David Nicholas, Gertrud Erbach, and Kevin Harris. *Journal of Information Science Principles & Practice*, v. 13, b. 2, p. 109, 1987.

"Overview of Online Databases, An" by Brendan Walsh. *Accountancy*, v. 96, p. 110, February 1986.

"Plague on Both Your Models, A" (information brokers and public libraries), by John Berry. *Library Journal* (LIBJA), p. 1355, July 1981.

"Productivity, Profit, and Libraries," by Leigh Estabrook. *Library Journal* (LIBJA), p. 1377, July 1981.

"Quality of Indexing in Online Data Bases," by Howard D. White and Belver C. Griffith. *Information Processing & Management* (UK), v. 23, n. 3, p. 211, 1987.

"Quiet Success of Videotex, The," by Hilary B. Thomas. *Association & Society Manager*, v. 19, n. 4, p. 18, June/July 1987.

"Re-use and Re-packaging of Information: The Information Intermediary Viewpoint," by Andrew P. Garvin. *Information Services Use*, 3(1/2), pp. 7–9, Spring 1983.

"Read My Mind: What Users Want from Online Information," by Lenore S. Ridgway. *IEEE Transactions on Professional Communication*, v. PC–30, n. 2, p. 87, June 1987.

"Searchers' Perceptions of Online Database Vendors," by Michael Halperin. *Special Libraries*, v. 74, 119(6), April 1983.

"Steven Livers' Service Gives Small Businesses a Way to Compare Their Ad Placement Strategies with Their Competitors," by Nancy Croft. *Nation's Business* (NBUSA), v. 7, p. 36, October 1986.

"Subject is: Business; an Update on Electronic Information Sources, The," by Katherine Ackerman. *American Libraries*, v. 18, p. 378, May 1987.

"Subject Searching in an Online Catalog," by Carolyn O. Frost. *Information Technology & Libraries*, n. 6, n. 1, p. 60, March 1987.

"Towards Expert Systems for the Selection of Search Keys," by Raya Fidel. *Journal of the American Society for Information Science*, v. 37, p. 37, January 1986.

"UTLAS to Use Info-Doc for Delivery Services." *Library Journal* (LIBJA), p. 313, February 15, 1984.

"Views on End-User Searching," by Marydee Ojala. *Journal of the American Society for Information Science*, v. 37, p. 197, July 1986.

"Washington Online" (U.S. Government and other information available through online databases), by Bill Hogan. *D&B Reports*, v. 36, p. 46, July/August 1987.

"Way to Export Success: How an Information Broker Can Help Exporter, The," by Deborah C. Sawyer. *Canadian Manager*, pp. 6–7, December 1982.

"What's New in On-Line Services," by Russ Lockwood. *Personal Computing*, v. 11, n. 6, p. 151, June 1987.

"Why are Online Catalogs Hard to Use? Lessons Learned from Information-Retrieval Studies," by Christine L. Borgman. *Journal of the American Society for Information Science*, v. 37, p. 387, November 1986.

"Work in the Information Age," by Arthur J. Cordell. *Futurist* (FUTUA), p. 12, December 1985.

Educational Resources

In addition to the training offered by the major database producers and vendors, there are places you can go for training in research and the library sciences without having to be in serious pursuit of a Master of Library Science degree (though if you are, that's OK). The number of programs will no doubt increase as time goes on, but these are the ones that were available in late 1987. An organization such as the Information Industry Association would be a good source of information on courses. The Special Libraries Association is developing a computer-assisted educational program for 1988. The list following gives particular emphasis to those courses of study that are available on an at-home or correspondence basis, for those of you who do not live near one of these institutions.

Brigham Young University
Administrator of Student Services
Independent Study
206 Harmon Continuing Education Building
Provo, UT 84604
(801) 378-2868

Graduate School USDA
Director of Correspondence Study
Room 1404, South Building
14th and Independence Avenue, SW
Washington, DC 20250
(307) 447-7123

Granton Institute of Technology
263 Adelaide St. W.
Toronto, Ontario M5H 1Y3
Canada

Indiana University
Director of Independent Study Program
Owen Hall
Bloomington, IN 47405
(812) 355-3693

Loyola University of Chicago
  Correspondence Study Division
  Lewis Towers 510
  620 N. Michigan Ave.
  Chicago, IL 60611
  (312) 670-3018

Ohio University Independent Study
  Tupper Hall 303
  Athens, OH 45701
  (614) 594-6721

Oklahoma State University
  Independent and Correspondence Study Department
  001 Classroom Bldg.
  Stillwater, OK 74078
  (405) 624-6390

University of Alabama
  Director of Independent Study
  Independent Study Department
  P.O. Box 2967
  University, AL 35486
  (205) 348-7642

University of Minnesota
  Department of Independent Study
  45 Wesbrook Hall
  77 Pleasant St. S.E.
  Minneapolis, MN 55455
  (612) 373-3256

University of Mississippi
  Department of Independent Study
  Yerby Center for Continuing Education
  University, MS 38677
  (601) 232-7313

University of New Mexico
  Continuing Education and Community Services
  805 Yale Blvd., N.E.
  Albuquerque, NM 87131
  (505) 277-2105

University of North Carolina at Chapel Hill
Division of Extension and Continuing Educations
201 Abernethy Hall 002A
Chapel Hill, NC 27514
(919) 962–1106

University of Pittsburgh
University External Studies Program
3808 Forbes Ave.
Pittsburgh, PA 15260

University of Tennessee
Center for Extended Learning
420 Communications and Extension Building
Knoxville, TN   996

University of Utah
1152 Annex
Salt Lake City, UT 84112
(801) 581–6472

University of Wyoming
Correspondence Study Department
Box 3294, University Station
Laramie, WY 82701
(307) 766–5631

Utah State University
Independent Study Division
Life Span Learning Program
Logan, UT 84322

Appendix

Database Suppliers' Responses on Copyright Questions

The following is a sampling of reply letters and forms received from database suppliers regarding the question of supplying the results of a database search by an independent contractor (the information broker) to a third party (the broker's client). This sample is hardly comprehensive, and even in so small a selection there is considerable variation in supplier policy. If you are at all in doubt about the legality of such a transaction for a particular database service, consult a competent attorney.

American Society of Hospital Pharmacists

4630 Montgomery Avenue
Bethesda, MD 20814

(301) 657-3000

September 30, 1987

Dear Mr. Everett:

I am writing in answer to your recent inquiry regarding International Pharmaceutical Abstracts in relation to the textbook manuscript you are preparing titled, The Information Broker's Handbook: How to Profit from the Information Age.

Yes, we do have a specific policy regarding third party searchers working for an independent client. I have enclosed a copy of our Letter of Agreement used for such a situation.

Good luck with your book. If I can provide further information, let me know.

Sincerely,

Dwight R. Tousignaut, Pharm.D., Editor
International Pharmaceutical Abstracts

DRT/nh/092305
Enclosure

License Agreement

The American Society of Hospital Pharmacists, Inc., 4630 Montgomery Avenue, Bethesda, MD 20814 is prepared to contract with _____ based upon the following terms and conditions:

Permission is given to electronically deliver the results of searches performed on International Pharmaceutical Abstracts data base.

Our permission is restricted to the following procedures:

1. Search results will be provided to clients as hard copy printout.

2. Searches will be done on a one time basis for each client.

3. There will be no alteration, reformatting or changing of the search results.

4. There will be no storage of search results beyond the time required to transmit to our client.

5. There will be no copying of searches or re-use of the search results.

6. Specific data base identification will be included for any IPA record that is part of a customized bibliography or search product. IPA terms and conditions (IPA is copyrighted and no further reproduction, duplication or sale of IPA records is permitted without written authorization from IPA--

limited reproduction of printed output up to 10 copies is permitted at the geographical site to which the information is delivered) must be transmitted with IPA records to clients.

It is our specific understanding that this permission involves only providing search results to clients, and that there will be no reformatting, copying or storage of search results beyond the time required to transmit.

ASHP will have the right to examine the operation of your transmitting procedure on request.

This Agreement can be terminated by written notice from either party.

This License constitutes the entire agreement between the parties and supersedes any and all written or oral prior agreements and understandings.

September 18, 1987

DISCLOSURE

5161 River Road
Bethesda, Maryland 20816
Telephone: 301-951-1300
Telex: 89-8452

Dear Mr. Everett:

Thank you for your interest in the Disclosure Database. I have enclosed for your review a copy of an article published in the Disclosure newsletter. The article discusses Disclosure's policies and practices concerning downloading. The article was first published about two years ago, but nothing has changed since that time.

Our policies for downloading information from Compact Disclosure parallel those for the various online systems. In other words, if the downloading and resupplying of the data is a one time occurrence, then Disclosure would generally grant the user (broker) permission. If however, the user (broker) is planning on downloading information for constant resale to their customers, Disclosure would want to negotiate a contract for royalties.

We do not at the present time have a preprinted contract explaining the details for reselling of the data. We rely primarily on the honesty of the customer to inform us at the time of leasing Compact Disclosure what their intent is to be. (I have enclosed a Compact Disclosure standard lease agreement, from which you may reprint the terms and conditions of use as they are state on the back of the contract.)

Please feel free to reprint any or all of the enclosed article or any of the above text. If there is anything I can do to clarify our policy, please do not hesitate to contact me at 301-951-1453. Again, thank you for your interest in including information on the Disclosure Database and Compact Disclosure.

Sincerely,

Susan Willner
Database Services

Enclosures

Dun's Marketing Services

DB a company of
The Dun & Bradstreet Corporation

Richard A. Itz
Manager
Online Products

49 Old Bloomfield Avenue, Mt. Lakes Corporate Center II
Mt. Lakes, NJ 07046
201-299-0181

September 11, 1987

Dear Mr. Everett:

This is in response to your letter requesting information about our copyright procedures. Our policy is stated on the front of our bluesheets. However, as an information broker you are allowed to run a search and charge your client. We prohibit you from making copies of that search and reselling it over and over again.

If you have further questions, please feel free to call me direct.

Sincerely,

Richard A. Itz

Richard A. Itz

RAI/po

BIOSIS
BIOSCIENCES
INFORMATION
SERVICE / Celebrating 60 Years of Service to the Biological Community

September 15, 1987

Dear Mr. Everett:

Thank you for your inquiry concerning the use of BIOSIS databases in connection with information brokerages.

Normally, information brokers are allowed to convey the results of a search to their clients without any special permission from us. Clients should be informed that no rights to republish such results are granted when such a service is provided.

With regard to downloading, as the enclosed BIOSIS Downloading Agreement states: Downloaded information may be freely used without further payment to BIOSIS when temporarily stored in lieu of hard copy or printout form which is the normal medium delivered by a vendor. Further, such temporarily stored information may be treated by user in such a manner as to rearrange, delete or revise without charge."

The other contingency would be if an information broker elected to provide search results in machine-readable form. This downloading activity also is covered in the enclosed Downloading Agreement, and if an information broker plans to use this approach, they should so indicate by signing it and returning it to us.

Sincerely,

Dena Gordon

Dena Gordon
Head,
User Services Department

DG/ss

Enclosures

cc: A. W. Elias

BIOSIS DOWNLOADING AGREEMENT

- **BACKGROUND**

   BioSciences Information Service (BIOSIS) prepares, publishes and distributes copyrighted information products available in printed form and from a number of computer services known as systems suppliers or VENDORS. The undersigned is a USER of one or more of these systems. This agreement defines the rights of BIOSIS and USER in normal and special uses of BIOSIS data based on a process known as "downloading".

- **DOWNLOADING**

   Downloading is a process through which the USER captures information on an electronic medium in whole or in part through a VENDOR system.

- **NORMAL DOWNLOADING RIGHTS**

   Downloaded information may be freely used without further payment to BIOSIS when *temporarily* stored in lieu of hard copy or printout form which is the normal medium delivered by a VENDOR. Further, such temporarily stored information may be treated by USER in such a manner as to rearrange, delete or revise without charge.

   It is the sense of this agreement that temporary storage/use ceases when USER alters the archival characteristic granted above and incorporates BIOSIS information into an active system of any type and in any form.

- **RESERVED RIGHTS**

   Downloaded information may be permanently held by USER in an active system in whole or in part upon payment of the following fees. Minimum order is 500 references.

ANNUAL FEE SCHEDULE

Number/Per Year	References(each)	References + Abstracts(each)
1-10,000	.15	.30
10,001-25,000	.10	.20
25,001-50,000	.05	.10
50,001-100,000	.035	.07

- **REPORTING AND PAYMENT**

   In consideration of this license for Reserved Rights, USER agrees to pay BIOSIS an amount equal to the product of the fees noted in FEE SCHEDULE and his estimate of the number of items to be taken for one (1) year from the effective date of this agreement.

   USER understands that advance payment is due each year based on the estimate. It is further understood that should the total number of items taken exceed the estimate and prepaid amounts, that BIOSIS will invoice USER for any amounts due at the applicable rate.

   USER further understands that due to the nature of the downloading process that BIOSIS totally relies on USER to provide reports of items in excess of the estimate. Such reports are due within thirty (30) days after the estimate is exceeded and monthly thereafter.

   No refunds will be made for overestimates.

   USER understands that the downloaded information may not be used at other than the site described herein without BIOSIS permission in writing.

   USER understands that he may make no electronic or other copy of the information obtained by downloading. A security copy may be held at the site described herein.

   USER understands that downloaded information may not be used for purposes of publication or database production in printed or other form, without the express written permission of BIOSIS.

- **TERMINATION**

   This agreement may be terminated on 60 days notice by either party. Refunds will be made on a pro rata basis.

- **TERM**

   The term of this agreement shall be one (1) year from the date of execution thereof. Downloading may begin on

   BIOSIS USE

   _____ LS
   Name

System Name/Acct. No.   **Downloading Location**

_____   Organization _____

_____   City _____

_____   State/Country _____ Zip/Postal Code _____

Vendor System(s) Used (Will be Held Confidential)
- -
DOWNLOADING ESTIMATE   Total No. _____

REFERENCES ONLY _____   REFERENCES + ABSTRACTS _____

Distribution of copies: *White* — BIOSIS   *Yellow* — Customer Service Copy   *Pink* — USER Copy

USER: Return all 3 copies to BIOSIS for billing purposes. A copy will be mailed to you after processing.

DOWNLOADING ESTIMATES

There are several approaches to projecting the quantities of BIOSIS items to be downloaded annually. These include using SDI yields if they are to be used to form an active data base, knowledge of individual users desires to accumulate search results, and corporate objectives in subject areas. Remember that downloading can be applied to both older and current files in making your estimates. Some general levels can be detected from the number of offline and online hits employed over a reasonable time period. If these approaches are impractical, consider placing the minimum estimate (500 items) and reporting the actual number used thereafter.

SAMPLE CALCULATION

Basis: Assume 12,000 candidate items for downloading:

A: **References Only:**

10,000 @ .15 each	=	$1,500.00	
2,000 @ .10 each	=	200.00	
12,000		$1,700.00	

B. **References + Abstracts**

10,000 × 60% = 6,000 (With Abstracts)	× .30 each	=	$1,800.00
4,000 (References Only)	× .15 each	=	600.00
10,000			$2,400.00
2,000 × 60% = 1,200 (With Abstracts)	× .20 each	=	$ 240.00
800 (References Only)	× .10 each	=	80.00
2,000			$ 320.00

Total	12,000	$2,720.00

Chemical Abstracts Service

A DIVISION OF THE AMERICAN CHEMICAL SOCIETY	2540 OLENTANGY RIVER ROAD P.O. BOX 3012 COLUMBUS, OHIO 43210	PHONE: 614-421-3600 TWX: 810-482-1608 CABLE: CHEMABS

September 24, 1987

Dear Mr. Everett:

In reply to your recent inquiry about Chemical Abstracts Service's policy regarding intermediary searchers working on behalf of independent clients, CAS views such intermediaries as individual searchers governed by the same constraints as any individual who searches CAS databases. Anyone who searches a CAS database on any online service must have a user agreement with the online service. While the form of the agreement may vary from service to service, the provisions applicable to CAS files are those stipulated in the License Agreement between CAS and the online service defining the conditions and limitations of use of CAS data. An excerpt from the pertinent section of the License Agreement is enclosed.

Under these conditions and limitations, an intermediary or broker may provide one printed copy of search results to a client so long as the American Chemical Society copyright notice appears on each page. The intermediary or broker may provide a single electronic copy of search results to a client if the client is an "Authorized User" of CAS data, i.e., has a formal agreement with an online service or with CAS to abide by the conditions and limitations of use stipulated by CAS. Distribution of results of a single search, in any form, to more than one client is an "Other Use" as defined in the License Agreement, and must be authorized by CAS.

CAS is willing to consider specific arrangements with individual brokers that may go beyond what is explicitly permitted under the License Agreement. However, we rigidly adhere to the principle that the ultimate user of the information--in this case, the broker's clients--must explicitly agree to the conditions and limitations of use specified in the License Agreement.

Sincerely,
CHEMICAL ABSTRACTS SERVICE

Edward P. Donnell
Senior Advisor, Corporate Communications

Enclosure

∨ EXCERPT FROM AMERICAN CHEMICAL SOCIETY
ONLINE LICENSE AGREEMENT

5. <u>CONDITIONS AND LIMITATIONS OF USE</u>

Licensee agrees to obtain from all Licensee Customers a binding commitment to abide by the following conditions and limitations:

5.1. <u>Individual Use.</u> Authorized Users may capture, retain, and use Licensed Data received from Licensee in any form and on any medium and for any period of time, provided that such Data are used exclusively by a single individual who is himself an Authorized User and are not made available to any third party.

5.2. <u>Distribution to Third Parties.</u> Absent explicit prior written authorization from CAS, Authorized Users may distribute Licensed Data only as follows:

5.2.1. for publication in a copyrighted scientific work, provided that such Licensed Data are incidental to the subject matter of the work;

5.2.2. for publication in reports to a government agency, provided that such reports and such Licensed Data are required by government rules, regulations, or law;

5.2.3. for one-time distribution of a single printed copy to a single individual, provided that the ACS Copyright Notice is included on every printed page; and,

5.2.4. for one-time distribution of a single electronic copy to a single individual, provided that said individual is an Authorized User, and provided that the ACS Copyright Notice is included at least once in each such distribution.

5.3. <u>Other Uses.</u> Should Authorized User wish to make use of Licensed Data except as permitted above, a request to do so may be submitted to CAS, who shall respond promptly and directly to said User. For example, Authorized Users who wish to capture search results in computer-readable form for electronic distribution to multiple individuals, to make printed copies of search results for distribution to multiple individuals, to permit third parties other than Authorized Users to gain access to CAS data, e.g., through gateway services, or to make any other use of such data not explicitly permitted above, may do so only upon securing appropriate authorization from CAS.

5.4. <u>Copyright and Ownership.</u> ACS retains all right, title, and interest in and to Licensed Data. User acquires no such right, title, or interest under this agreement.

-2-

Pertinent Definitions

    3.2. <u>Authorized Customer</u>. A Licensee Customer who has agreed to abide by the conditions and limitations of use as set forth in Section 5.

    3.3. <u>Authorized User</u>. A User who is an Authorized Customer or any User who is a bona fide employee or agent of an Authorized Customer or of Licensee and who is acting within the scope of a formal employment or agency relationship.

**INFORMATION
ACCESS
COMPANY**

11 Davis Drive
Belmont, California 94002
415/591-2333
800/227-8431

September 18, 1987

Dear Mr. Everett:

Information Access Company's policy regarding use of its
databases by information brokers is as follows:

- IAC allows information brokers to provide clients with
  search results so long as

  1) the same search results are not reproduced and
     distributed to multiple clients and
  2) the client is provided with only one copy of search
     results

- Search results given to the client must include the
  following copyright statement:

  © Information Access Company, Belmont, California

- Clients must be notified that copies of the search results
  may not be reproduced and distributed without Information
  Access Company's permission.

You may include this information in your textbook. Please call
me if you have questions about this policy.

Sincerely,

Susan O. Higgins
Online Marketing Manager

SOH:jlr

a division of Ziff-Davis Publishing Company

△⚊ Arthur D. Little Decision Resources

Acorn Park
Cambridge. Massachusetts 02140–2390
617 864-5770 Telex 921436

September 16, 1987

To Whom It May Concern:

I apologize for the salutation, but I misplaced your letter requesting information about our policy on use of our database, Arthur D. Little/OnLine, by third-party information brokers. (I did, however, retrieve your envelope from the circular file.)

We have a number of information brokers who use our file and are pleased to have them as customers. To those who request permission to conduct third-party searches in our file, we send the following statement of our policy.

> The results of searches done on behalf of your clients are not to be included in any compilation made available for sale, except as you make a single such compilation for a single client. All such printouts are to be clearly marked as to the source -- i.e., Arthur D. Little/OnLine. In addition, search results are not to be further reproduced or disseminated within your client's organization.

> Our policy regarding downloading from our database allows users to download for purposes of editing, reformatting, etc. We do not allow permanent storage on disks, nor do we allow multiple disks to be made from our file. Should your client wish to purchase a document as a result of searching our file, we would want to fulfill that order ourselves.

> While it is true that "no one owns a fact," please note that our database contains more than "facts." It contains the judgment, opinions, insights, and forecasts of our Arthur D. Little staff. As such, we <u>do own</u> this information.

> Therefore, we cannot allow you to "use, analyze, extract, process and re-work" our material. Each record you take from our file must be delivered to your client in its <u>entirety</u> with clear indications as to the source and ownership of the information contained therein.

Amsterdam	Mexico City	Sao Paulo
Brussels	Milan	Singapore
Houston	New York	Tokyo
London	Paris	Toronto
Los Angeles	Riyadh	Washington
Madrid	San Francisco	Wiesbaden

/IL Arthur D. Little Decision Resources

September 16, 1987
Page two

We do not have any specific forms for information brokers to complete.

For your information, I am enclosing copies of our recent newsletters to give you some background on our database.

Thank you for mentioning our file in your forthcoming book. If you have any further questions, please don't hesitate to call me.

Sincerely,

Anne V. Quinn
Director, Arthur D. Little/OnLine

AVQ/jj

Encl.

11001 Cedar Avenue, Cleveland, Ohio 44106
800-321-6388   (216) 795-3000   Telex: 985 604

September 24, 1987

Re: Your letter requesting policy on re-selling of PROMT
     information

Dear Mr. Everett,

You requested the above captioned information in preparation for
a manuscript you intend to publish.

On the subject of "third party intermediary searchers working on
behalf of independent clients" we do permit intermediaries to
resell Predicasts database information to individual clients for
proprietary use. All copyright protections and restrictions
apply, including those expressly stated in Predicasts Downloading
Policy (copy attached).

If you have further questions, please call me.

                                     Sincerely,
                                     Predicasts

                                     Gordon Lensner
                                     Director; Marketing

GL::
encl.

11001 Cedar Avenue, Cleveland, Ohio 44106
800-321-6388   (216) 795-3000   Telex: 985 604

PREDICASTS DOWNLOADING POLICY

Predicasts authorizes the downloading of data from the PTS database(s) to an in-house microcomputer(s), word processor(s), or other storage device(s). Downloading is defined as the movement of information in machine-readable form to an in-house storage device for the purpose of editing, merging, reformatting, and/or storing the information for future use. Use of the downloaded information is limited to periodic searches of the resulting database. Customer agrees that the data downloaded from the PTS database(s) shall be used for internal or in-house purposes only and shall not be disseminated to any other organization or used for commercial purposes. The downloaded data may not be duplicated in hard-copy or machine-readable form without written authorization from Predicasts, except that limited reproduction of printed hard-copy output of up to five (5) copies is permitted for internal distribution.

Permission requests should be sent to Predicasts, 11001 Cedar Avenue, Cleveland, Ohio, 44106, Attention: Online Services.

Index